COMMON SENSE FOR A PROSPEROUS LIFE

BOOK 1

RICHES BEYOND THE BLING

Clear Thinking on Money, Financial Independence and Life's True Riches

Mark Ashe

RICHES BEYOND THE BLING © 2021, 2026
by Mark Ashe. All rights reserved.

Published by Author Academy Elite
PO Box 43, Powell, OH 43065
www.AuthorAcademyElite.com

All rights reserved. This book contains material protected under international and federal copyright laws and treaties. Any unauthorized reproduction, distribution, transmission, display, or use of this material is prohibited.

No part of this book may be reproduced or transmitted in any form or by any means, electronic or mechanical, including photocopying, recording, scanning, scraping, or by any information storage and retrieval system, without the express prior written permission of the author.

Without limiting the author's exclusive rights under copyright law, no part of this work may be reproduced, copied, extracted, scraped, ingested, analyzed, or used for the purpose of training, fine-tuning, developing, or improving artificial intelligence systems, machine learning models, or generative models—whether commercial or non-commercial—without the author's prior written consent.

The author expressly reserves all rights to license this work for any AI-related uses.

Identifiers:
LCCN: 2020912944
ISBN: 978-1-64746-388-5 (paperback)
ISBN: 978-1-64746-389-2 (hardback)
ISBN: 978-1-64746-390-8 (ebook)

Available in paperback, hardback, e-book

Scripture quotations marked (NIV) are taken from the Holy Bible, New International Version®, NIV®. Copyright © 1973, 1978, 1984, 2011 by Biblica, Inc.® Used by permission of Zondervan. All rights reserved worldwide. www.zondervan.com The "NIV" and "New International Version" are trademarks registered in the United States Patent and Trademark Office by Biblica, Inc.®

Scripture taken from the New King James Version®. Copyright © 1982 by Thomas Nelson. Used by permission. All rights reserved.

Scripture quotations marked (NLT) are taken from the Holy Bible, New Living Translation, copyright ©1996, 2004, 2015 by Tyndale House Foundation. Used by permission of Tyndale House Publishers, a Division of Tyndale House Ministries, Carol Stream, Illinois 60188. All rights reserved.

Cover design by Perry Yeldham, 21Thirteen Design, Inc.
perry@21thirteen.com

Other Books by Mark Ashe

The *Common Sense for a Prosperous Life* series

Invest Like a Wealth Manager
The Entry-Level CEO
Unchain Your Brain
Private Choices, Public Power

People who are down and out financially are down and out mentally. They are suffering from a mental disease of discouragement and loss of hope....
They have lost their way on the life path and need to be shown the way back.

—Orison Swett Marden

CONTENTS

Author's Notes ix

Chapter 1—Financial Independence vs. Wealth 1
Chapter 2—How to Achieve Financial Independence 6
       Thirteen Keys to Financial Independence . . . 8

Chapter 3—Margin Instead of Debt 11
       Your New Mindset 14

       Impulse Purchases 16

       Quit Digging Yourself into a Hole 20

       Don't Be a Penny Pincher 25

       High Income Does Not Mean High
       Financial IQ. 26

Chapter 4—The Proper Use of Credit 28
       The Importance of Reading, Prayer, and
       Active Faith 29

       Faith Without Works Is Dead 32

       Thoughts on Debt 34

Guidelines for Borrowing 36

Chapter 5—Progress Requires a Written Plan 40
    Learning the Fundamentals 41

    Emotional Investment 42

    Your Plan 46

Chapter 6—Financial Plan 1 47
    Should You Read This? 48

    An Explanation of the Tithe Principle 49

    And So, I Started 52

    Not a Trick 55

    The Bottom Line of Why I Tithe 56

    But Where Should the Tithe Go? 64

    Putting to Work the Law of Increase 71

Chapter 7—Financial Plans 2 and 3 75
    Where All Wealth Starts 76

    Savings Must Be Kept in a Separate Account 78

    Medical 80

    Life 80

    Disability 82

    A Reminder of the Importance of Plans
    1, 2, and 3 82

Chapter 8—Financial Plans 4, 5, and 6 86
Chapter 9—Financial Plans 7 and 8. 95
        My Rationale for Paying Off Your Home. . . 98

        Answers to Some Common Questions. . . . 104

        Riches Greater Than Money 108

        Waking Up Not Owing a Dime! 113

        Getting the Things You Want 117

Chapter 10—Beyond the Bling 119
        How Long It Took 119

        Absence of Debt = Financial
        Independence? 121

        Taking on Debt on Purpose 123

        Paying Tuition for a Hard Lesson 126

        Your Choice: Excuses or Progress? 127

        Now What? 130

        Your Decision: One Step at a Time 132

Chapter 11—My Final Thoughts. 134
        What are the True Riches
        Beyond the Bling 135

About the Author 136

AUTHOR'S NOTES

As I sit in my study, I am looking at a framed photograph of Orison Swett Marden. Mr. Marden wrote a lot in the late 1800s about character and its relationship to wealth. He was orphaned as a young boy and put out to hard labor as little more than a slave. Overworked and underfed, he was often beaten by a tyrannical master. Half-starving most of the time, he would sneak an extra bite of food when he found it, terrified of the beating he would receive if he were caught. With no one to aid him, encourage him, guide him—or even love him—he yet *lifted himself* to become one of the preeminent authors of his time. He wrote with authority on the subject of rising from limiting circumstances to achieve a satisfying place in life.

After submitting his first book, *Pushing to the Front,* to several publishers—unsure if any would be willing to print it—to his surprise, publishers actually fought each other over the rights to the book. That book was reprinted again and again and distributed around the globe! Governments bought the book for nationwide distribution in their schools.

In a later book, *Good Manners: A Passport to Success*, Mr. Marden penned twenty-seven words that set the course of my adult life:

> ***It is the duty of every young person, and especially of every young man, to set about the task of becoming financially independent. The amount is inconsequential.***

From the first time I read those words, now thirty-five years ago, those two sentences became my personal philosophy—and my obsession. They became my life's field manual and I began a passionate pursuit to attain financial independence.

Even though I still am not a financial sophisticate or a business tycoon (or even had those things as goals), by the age of forty-five I lived on a beautiful farm in the foothills of the North Georgia mountains and I was debt-free and financially independent. My wife and children were living a blessed life, and I was there with them to enjoy every day of it.

Armies issue their new soldiers a "field manual." When faced with a decision, a soldier can go to the manual, refer to the appropriate section, and see quickly what to avoid and what course of action to take to increase the odds of a desirable outcome. I have long been of the opinion that, if a practical reference manual could be written for making the major decisions of life—especially if written in an engaging style—a great need would be met for us civilians fighting the battles of life.

To that end, I have written the Common Sense for a Prosperous Life book series, five quick-read handbooks that cut straight to the heart of the most important issues of life:

1. earning and spending,

2. saving and investing,

3. running a business,

AUTHOR'S NOTES

4. creative thinking, intention, and focus, and

5. mature judgment, marriage, and other personal choices.

But I chose to write these books—including the one you now hold in your hand—with great reluctance. Here's how it happened.

In 2008 I witnessed the global financial meltdown that would shake the world's markets for years, but I had seen it coming. Almost all of the "prosperity" everyone seemed to be enjoying leading up to the crash was an illusion built on excessive debt and other bad decisions.

During those earlier years of society-wide excessive borrowing and spending, an unbidden idea kept pushing itself up, forcing its way into my mind. The thought seemed preposterous, an errant notion passing through the wrong mind, and, at first, I treated it exactly like that. Over time, however, it grew into a conviction that I could not escape, even as I continued to thrust it away.

Here is that thought:

> *Mark, you write a book that will give the reader a healthy foundation for decisions concerning money, business, and personal life. This current foolishness—the "You can get rich quick and live rich now; here's how!" mantra being fed to the unsophisticated and gullible public by new money magazines, how-I-got-rich authors, and breathless news anchors on financial channels excitedly reporting the day's Wall Street winners—must be confronted.*

> *The healthy intention to become an independent, balanced, self-restrained adult has been lost. Independence, not consumption, must once again be held up for all to see as the proper purpose of labor. You are to write a book that will spell out, in simple terms, a practical mindset toward money,*

business, and life that will provide a road map to help ordinary men and women see clearly to make wiser choices.

As I have said, I repeatedly dismissed this most unwelcome impulse. After many years of hard work in my own business, I had no appetite for such a time-consuming task, nor did I feel competent. Not only did I feel unqualified to write about these things—after all, my accomplishments are modest when compared to those of the wealthy best-selling authors so prevalent on bookshelves—but I did not believe I had any gift at all for writing, on *any* subject. I did not want, nor have I ever desired, to write a book.

For several years, I continued to consider the thought ridiculous. Then I had a health scare that turned out to be a false alarm. But this was the turning point for me. Why? Because the first thought that went through my mind when I feared bad news was not for myself or my family. To my shock, it was instead, "I should have written that book."

That's when I realized this work was something I *must* do, I was *intended* to do, whether or not I thought it reasonable. And, even before I returned the call to the doctor's office, I made up my mind that I would begin.

In 2010—after nearly a decade of my hard work—*Your Money & Your Life: A Guide to Building Character and Capital* was published. The feedback I got was that it was fantastic, but so varied in topics and filled with good information that it would've been helpful to be more subject-specific.

So, I went back to work for a few more years, and now you have in your hand the result—one volume in a five-book series called *Common Sense for a Prosperous Life*. One way or another, the writing of these books has taken much of my time for nearly eighteen years, and, at this moment, I still have no idea if this series will ever see the light of day. But I do know this much: books such as these are needed *badly*, and, if these

AUTHOR'S NOTES

books are ever published, everyone who reads them will be better off because they will finish every book with far greater clarity of thought for decision making on the subjects that determine quality of life.

Only a fortunate few are born into this world with a "wealth consciousness"—a mind that expects or creates wealth—or gifted with a highly marketable talent. The rest of us have to devote a great deal of our time to earning money and deciding how our very limited resources should be used. The Common Sense for a Prosperous Life series was written to give just this sort of reader a mature and sensible mindset toward all kinds of money matters, and also a blueprint for conquering our private demons and making personal choices that are as clear as "Follow the yellow brick road."

Let me begin by stating the obvious. For all but the truly wealthy, building a comfortable life will require several things:

- You must handle whatever you earn deliberately, so it does not slip away.
- You must earn more money than is required for food, clothing, shelter, and other living expenses (which, I admit, is increasingly difficult to do).
- You must not be careless with the money you save.
- You must overcome your own internal hindrances.
- You must not forfeit your progress to an undisciplined private life.

By the time you have finished reading this series, you will have a road map for the five "musts" above.

Book 1—*Riches Beyond the Bling: Clear Thinking on Money, Financial Independence and Life's True Riches* reveals how to handle the money you earn, purposefully.

Book 2—*Invest Like a Wealth Manager: Simplify Your Thinking to Invest Your Money with Confidence* gives you my own common-sense guidelines for saving and investing.

Book 3—*The Entry-Level CEO: Simple Secrets to Build a Profitable Business (Even with No Experience!)* is ideal for those with a desire to work for themselves. It relates some thoughts on increasing your income by building a business of your own.

Book 4—*Unchain Your Brain: Move Beyond Fear and Discouragement and Start Living with Purpose* delivers a powerful read for overcoming fear and discouragement and moving you toward your next goal.

Book 5—*Private Choices, Public Power: Personal Decisions that Determine Your Destiny* is the fifth and final book in the series, is filled with practical help regarding personal issues, which, if handled carelessly, can wreck a life.

None of these books is a sermon, and they are not boring—I promise. I believe every page will grip you with its practical and immediate common sense. Pick up any of the books, open them anywhere, read three pages, and I trust you will not want to quit reading from right where you are. To my mind, that is the test of a well-written and worthy book: there is no place in it that does not quickly engage the reader on a personal level.

The lessons contained within are timeless. They will be just as helpful to a reader sixty years from now as today. So, if you are a parent and you can read this book without considering it imperative to set aside a copy for each of your children, I have

AUTHOR'S NOTES

failed. If you are a wife and you can read this book without insisting that your husband also read it, I have failed.

I truly believe you will not toss these aside: I am *that* confident that the five books in the *Common Sense for a Prosperous Life* series have no substitute in the marketplace. Having read hundreds of such books myself, I believe these are among those rare works immediately useful to every reader in every generation.

Welcome to my major life assignment, my best effort to make the world a better place by giving the reader practical instruction for the most important issues of life.

Choose well and prosper.

Mark Ashe
Gainesville, Georgia
2020

CHAPTER 1
FINANCIAL INDEPENDENCE VS. WEALTH

Financial independence is a healthy and prudent objective for everyone.

Clear thinking and money are required for everything you and I need to sustain our lives with dignity. The air we breathe is free, but we need money for everything else—everything, even water. As much as I disdain any man who makes a god of a dollar bill, I have no less contempt for the financial fool. Millions of adults, particularly men, through selfish decisions or lack of mature judgment, sentence themselves and their families to a worry-filled life that eventually wears away the joys of marriage and home.

Almost every person upon entering active life sets out with an intention to own his or her own home, to become debt-free, and to live without needless stress. That is, to become financially independent.

Few make it.

Such an accomplishment requires departures from the norm in the choices one makes. The things we value must be different, for it is what the heart truly values that decides for us when weighing choices. What you are about to be invited to experience through reading my words is the birthing of a dream for your own independence. I will encourage you to develop a compelling desire to be free of the burden of debts.

From the very outset, no matter how bleak your current situation feels, I boldly state that **you should set a definite goal to become financially independent**. This goal is the proper objective for *everyone*, no matter how impossible it may seem, and no matter what your current income.

This goal is not about an unwholesome obsession with money. No, making up your mind to become an independent adult is inherently wholesome, safe, and life-building. It develops the man or woman without deceiving him or her. To become rich is not a reasonable goal for everyone, but the dignity of financial independence is.

It is human nature to exaggerate the value of things we don't have, but the value of living with no worried thoughts about bills—a stress-free life—cannot be exaggerated. I know. Having planned, worked, and sacrificed for it for years, and having now lived it for many years, I can say with certainty, it is as worthwhile as we all imagine it to be.

Now, I am not talking about luxury cars and mansions; I don't have those things myself, nor do I want the care of them. I am talking about the highest form of wealth—a life of ceaseless mental peace.

Financial Independence vs. Wealth

If you have read the Author's Notes of this book—and I hope you have—you will recognize the name Orison Swett Marden, and know what an influence this nineteenth-century author has had on my life. In his book, *The Miracle of Right Thought*, Mr. Marden wrote a few lines that convincingly address the importance of financial independence:

FINANCIAL INDEPENDENCE VS. WEALTH

No man has a right, unless he cannot help himself, to remain where he will be constantly subjected to the cramping, ambition blighting influences and great temptations of poverty. His self-respect demands that he should get out of such an environment. It is his duty to put himself in a position of dignity and independence, where he will not be liable at any moment to be a burden to his friends in case of sickness or other emergencies, or where those depending on him may suffer.

And let me repeat the quote (again, please read my Author's Notes) from Mr. Marden that changed my life:

It is the duty of every young person, and especially of every young man, to set about the task of becoming financially independent. The amount is inconsequential.

Please fix your attention on the last sentence:

The amount is inconsequential.

That last sentence is a contradiction of the prevailing and harmful attitude that how much money you have is the measure of human achievement. Such an attitude about money will weaken rather than strengthen character. The pursuit of money for its own sake can corrupt priorities and adversely affect financial and moral judgments. Plenty of evidence of that was seen in the financial collapse of 2007–2010 as one reckless banking executive after another went to Washington and Brussels seeking tax dollars to save them, and one "investment" swindler after another was led away in handcuffs.

What does rich mean anyway? No matter how much we have, rich always seems to be the next level up from us, doesn't it? But an ample home filled with contentment, the companionship of a happy family, a little money set aside for emergencies, and the respect of those who know you best—that is priceless.

A few years ago, I was having a conversation with a dignified, elderly woman about some routine business issues. I don't remember how it was that this was brought into the conversation, but, at some point in our exchange, she told me with justifiable pride that she had never accepted a dime of welfare and had taught her children to disdain it. She then told me she and her husband had put four children through college in the rural South in the 1960s.

A bit awestruck, I asked her how they did that, suspecting she or her husband must have been a rare, high-income-earning African American professional before the success of civil rights. But that was not the case.

She said,

> I was a schoolteacher, and I did some private tutoring and also took in laundry. My husband was a mechanic. We lived within our means, saved our money, and stayed out of debt. My husband passed on a few years ago, but we have owned our own home outright for many years now, and I live just fine.

Rather overwhelmed with admiration, I asked out of curiosity how her children turned out. She said, "My sons are all professional men, and my daughter is married to one."

I am humbled by just relating that story. Anyone who has good health, and a job has no excuse for not attempting to gain the dignity that this woman earned—and passed on to her children. How pathetic a money-grasping man or woman would appear in the presence of such dignity and accomplishment!

The possession of large sums of money cannot possibly be a reliable measure of human worth. *But honestly won financial independence is always a reliable sign of value.* The true and lasting riches of dignity and independence go far beyond the "bling" of jewelry, fashion, cars, and homes. Yes, your own independence is the proper goal. If wealth comes in the process—and more often than we think possible when we begin, some degree of it will—it is then in proper hands.

And unless you are one of the few who come into sudden wealth, is it not obvious that financial independence *must* precede wealth?

When you focus your thoughts upon using every means possible to gain financial independence, you are simply learning the disciplines necessary to handle the higher levels of wealth that can come to you afterward.

But, when the only goal is to "be rich" or "make lots of money," there can be a loss of balance, in morals and in business judgment, which ends up being the ruin of the man. The events of 2007 and 2008 clearly exposed the results of greed for gains at any cost on a horrendous global scale. It was not the first time excess caused a tragic meltdown and sadly, it will not be the last.

Even though financial independence can be seen as a stepping-stone toward other things, the very nature of the intention to become independent and self-reliant (as opposed to becoming rich) brings stability to the thought process, and that naturally yields maturity and self-restraint. Financial independence is not enough cash set aside to last a lifetime; that is wealth. Financial independence is a life of contentment with no unmet needs.

Bottom line: **financial independence is a healthy and prudent objective for everyone**. So, how can you achieve it? In your hands is the roadmap that will answer that question by discussing how to handle the money you earn, purposefully.

Let's begin.

CHAPTER 2

HOW TO ACHIEVE FINANCIAL INDEPENDENCE

When money in the bank is hard to come by, don't buy things you can do without.

When I was a young man, perhaps nineteen years of age, I met a man of wealth. I had never been around anyone who had much money, and it occurred to me he did not seem superhuman. So, I reasoned, if he could make something out of his life, I might be able to make something out of mine.

I knew it might be harder for me than for someone with a college education or an upper-class background, but, for the first time, I began to think I was not just going to drift through life. I was going to try to amount to something.

At the time, I was a law enforcement specialist in the United States Air Force, stationed at Tinker Air Force Base in Oklahoma City. In other words, I was the base policeman. I finished out my enlistment and afterwards took a job as a civilian police officer in my home state of Georgia, all the while trying to think of some way to go into business.

HOW TO ACHIEVE FINANCIAL INDEPENDENCE

With little more in the way of qualifications than a lot of persistence and some common sense, I eventually became financially independent—though it took about twenty-seven years from when the thought first occurred to me at nineteen years of age. I had no advantages other than some basic good judgment about money, a fierce determination to live free from debt, and an unshakable commitment to be in business for myself. That was enough for me to become independent by my mid-forties.

Today, I live a blessed life and I am so grateful for it. I am well-aware an unseen hand came to my aid, as it could have turned out very differently. With absolutely no arrogance, I can say truthfully that I am living the life most people hope for, and I am about to list in just thirteen simple steps how I did it.

This list of financial precepts goes straight to the heart of every financial decision you will ever make. It is my personal list—what I might call *Thirteen Keys to Financial Independence*—and there is nothing on it requiring a single day of formal education. And you can submit these guidelines for review to the wealthiest man or woman you know, and they will tell you how valuable they are.

Whether you are driving a police car, as I was, or working at any other common occupation, if you will apply these rules to your own life, you will begin to think with purpose and act according to a long-term plan. I suggest you guide your household by these thirteen principles and teach them to your children.

These Thirteen Keys alone are worth more to you than you paid for this book—or all my books combined. If the only thing you take from reading my words is a commitment to the thoughts that follow…if you copy them and paste them on your mirror…if you begin to live by them…within a few years, you will significantly improve the emotional and financial well-being of your life.

I submit them to you for your earnest consideration.

Thirteen Keys to Financial Independence

1. You can't have things *and* money.
2. Money is a health issue. *Ready money is a health issue.*
3. It is not equally within everyone's power to earn money, but it is equally within everyone's power to save a portion of what they earn. Savings should not be less than 10 percent of your net income. Saving is not something you do with extra money; it is a personal lifestyle choice.
4. The tithe is the first and the best investment.
5. Do not spend money you have not yet earned.
6. When you think you want something—wait a year. If you still want it after one year, it is worth adding to your goals list. If the desire for it has passed (which will usually be the case), you have saved yourself from a wasteful expense. When money in the bank is hard to come by, don't buy things you can do without.
7. When deciding on the purchase of a home, consider it for what it really is: a large, money-consuming liability and a constant expense. And don't pay retail for a house. Find a motivated seller or a fixer-upper you can improve with your own efforts. Renting while you build savings is not foolish; it's smart.
8. You must earn more than is required for food, clothing, and shelter. Find ways to increase your income-producing ability. If the thought appeals to you, look for a way to work for yourself.

9. Don't trust good investment stories. If the profits were really certain, no one would be telling *you* about it. Hope is bait for fools. Never invest in anything you do not personally understand.

10. Beyond savings, invest a good portion of your money in things that give immediate guaranteed return or have intrinsic value: start your own business, pay off your debts or mortgage, buy some real estate or buy gold and silver when the prices of these assets are depressed. Limit the size of any speculative investments.

11. Don't be gullible or naïve. When it comes to your money, do not believe anyone is really thinking of your interests instead of seeking their own benefit from your dollars. Never invest money with anyone who solicits you first. Never!

12. Seek financial mentors and do not make serious money decisions without counsel. Choose mentors from men and women who have nothing to gain from your decisions.

13. Grow in personal and financial competence. Read a few minutes daily to reinforce your focus and listen to recordings that motivate you to be your best.

By reading and applying these thirteen guidelines—all of which will be expanded upon within *Riches Beyond the Bling* and the other books in my *Common Sense for a Prosperous Life* series—you can justify or negate every expense you are considering and avoid a host of mistakes.

Remember: by the application of these principles, I became financially independent relatively early in life, though I followed an unremarkable career path from enlisted military to a civilian policeman to a roofing contractor to home improvement contractor (and, hopefully, to successful author).

Yes, I was often discouraged by my slow progress. However, as my modest income grew, I had rules to do the right things with that money, rules I am sharing with you now for far less than the cost of a single meal. When you can purchase a lifetime of financial wisdom for less than ten dollars…that reader, is a great investment. By buying this book you have begun investing in your future…in your life!

The result was that most of the money I earned during those years did not slip away. Instead of being consumed, misspent, or lost to foolish investments, my money was constantly being pushed forward into my future in order to use its compounding power to fulfill my major objective—financial independence!

But, before I lay out specifics on the Thirteen Keys I have just shared with you, we need to take a look at the greatest single threat to achieving that independence—consumer debt.

CHAPTER 3
MARGIN INSTEAD OF DEBT

It takes a new mindset to overcome money's resistance to being held.

None of us can know what will come tomorrow. Each day, each twenty-four-hours is an inconsequentially short period of time relative to all the possibilities life may bring to us. In truth, neither you nor I know what will happen to us just five minutes from now.

So, in absolute terms, it is not within the power of any human being to control the events of his or her own life. For this reason, every responsible man or woman should make it a priority to build into their lives **margin**: a financial buffer for safety, to absorb some of the shock in the event of sudden changes.

Think of it this way. Suppose I offered you a new home, completely paid for—*if* you would get on a motorcycle and ride it at night, as fast as you could, on a curvy, busy road you had never driven, without any ability to see what was coming around the next curve. Would you do it?

What if, to be fair, I also warned you there was a place the road was washed out and you would encounter at least one careless driver who would come across the center line into your lane—and I still wanted you to drive as fast as you could? Would you do it for a free home?

It might be tempting, but I doubt you would. More likely, you would mull it over and conclude, "You're crazy! You must be nuts! You're talking about my life! No material thing, not even a home, could possibly be worth taking that much risk. That isn't even a calculated risk; it is just acting stupid." And, of course, that response is the only rational one.

Well, consider this, although your life is not at stake when you make financial decisions such as signing a thirty-year note for a home, the *quality* of your life most definitely is. *When making any financial commitment, your emotional health is at risk*, often for many years to come.

I can assure you, there *are* obstacles in the road of life ahead of you. That's a non-negotiable part of living. Hazards will appear without any regard for your financial readiness. They come to all of us. Most will be minor, like replacing a dishwasher. Some will be substantial, like an automobile needing a major repair. And some will be shocking, like the sudden loss of a job, a business collapse, or an illness.

When it comes to our money, we are each free to make decisions that either add to our safety or pile up debts as we go along. When you are considering a purchase and the thought comes, "I can make that payment," or "By the time the bill comes due, I'll have the money," does it occur to you just how much you are presuming?

You are presuming that, for the length of the loan, all your tomorrows will be just like today, if not better. Those presumptions, often one piled on top of the other—or the absence of them—will determine the quality of your financial and emotional life.

Quality of life is determined by *margin*, not by the things you possess. Keeping a comfortable margin for the unexpected in your financial decisions leaves your soul some elbowroom when encountering the unexpected events that will come to every life.

If you *plan* for unknown events, if you leave plenty of *margin* for them in your planning, you can remove much or all of their power to harm you when they arrive. But, if you presume each day will go along just as you think it will, you have given fickle circumstances a great deal of power over you.

On Bloomberg Television, I once heard an investment manager asked for his opinion about spending trends in the United States. He said, "One thing you can always count on: the typical American is going to spend all the money he has and all he can borrow." The statistics often seem to prove his cynical response was accurate. I was watching a roundtable discussion of economists on a Sunday news show several years ago and was startled when one of them commented that the national rate of savings for the citizens of the United States at that time was negative—less than zero.

I have found from my own experience that stress is **not** an automatic consequence of life. Rather, it usually results from financial pressures. Consumer debts and large house payments will remove options, safety, and peace from your life for decades at a time—*decades*! Every time you take on a debt, you are figuratively driving that motorcycle faster, closer to losing control, and nearer to oncoming traffic.

Of course, most of us will have some debt. But, when weighing any financial decision, I try to keep in mind that no material thing is worth more than my peace of mind.

We would all be better off if we realized that our quality of life—the very happiness we all desire—is a matter of **emotional peace**. It does not and cannot come from the price of our automobile or a home that meets every preference. Those things are pleasures worth working toward, but not at the expense of our soul-protecting margin.

We have all heard it said that money cannot buy health, but that is misleading. *There is one thing in life that promotes health and is, in fact, the only thing more valuable than your health and that is* **Peace of Mind.** And ready money can absolutely provide a good deal of that.

In other words, *financial margin equals mental and emotional health.*

> *More happiness is lost from the cost of living high than from the high cost of living.*
>
> —*Orison Swett Marden*

Your New Mindset

Here is the first fact about the nature of money I want you to grasp:

Money resists being held or accumulated.

Money is slippery. That is its nature. It flows quickly through and away from undisciplined hands. That's why the majority of people have no money saved, even though they've been earning it for years.

It takes a new mindset to overcome money's resistance to being held. Here is the mindset that will help overcome money's resistance to *you*:

1. You develop an emotional *need* to be financially independent.
2. You work, with equal vigor, to increase income *and* decrease expenses.
3. You control discretionary spending. You can say no to yourself and often do. You have a system for controlling purchases that prevent spending on impulse.

4. You have a written plan for where the money will go *before you earn it.*

5. You are properly insured against life's contingencies with life insurance (if you have dependents), medical insurance, and if you can afford it, disability insurance.

6. You are as excited about paying off a loan early as others are when they buy something new.

7. You can keep your hands off your growing amount of set-aside funds.

8. You know how to hang on to money and not lose it through foolishly overreaching for profits or falling for the deceptions of convincing promoters. Money will flee from anyone who naïvely entrusts it to the control of others or pursues impossible earnings with it. Much more on this in my second book in this series, *Invest Like a Wealth Manager.*

9. You invest your excess capital only when you personally understand what you are doing.

10. You understand it is your responsibility to get out of consumer debt, and you keep yourself focused on this by regularly dipping into a good book on the subject. *Riches Beyond the Bling* will do.

I would suggest you read this list again, but now out loud. There is something about speaking an important thought out loud that just makes a difference in the lasting impression it has on us. And, by the way, you'll be learning much more about all these qualities of your new mindset as you continue to read. This is how you lay the foundation for security and wealth. Because, as you prepare yourself to retain and manage money, an increase in your income can more easily follow. A person constantly stressed out over money is in a poor state of mind to attract more of it.

Therefore, if you want to get into a bigger dollar league than you're in now, the first step is to learn to delay obtaining any material thing *until you have earned it*. When you have truly earned something, there will not be much in the way of ego involved in the purchase. You won't need to call attention to it, and you won't need it to call attention to you. It will just fit you.

And that brings us to our next point of discussion: *how do you keep more of your money?* We begin by talking about learning to identify and delay those unearned expenditures.

Impulse Purchases

For years, I have followed a rule of avoiding *all* impulse purchases. Here's how I have done it.

Whenever anything I wanted—not needed—cost, say, more than a few hundred dollars, I wrote it down, but I did not allow myself to buy it right away. Now, what I am about to say may seem severe, but it worked flawlessly for me and had three essential components.

1. If it cost more than a few hundred dollars, I would not allow myself to buy it for one year.

If, after one year, I still wanted it, then it was a legitimate purchase. It was no longer even possible it was wasteful or impulsive. But that did *not* mean after the year had passed, I allowed myself to go right out and buy it.

2. Once that waiting test had been passed, I then set the purchase as an incentive for meeting a goal.

In other words, I had to accomplish something on my long-term goal list before I could reward myself with the purchase.

In the beginning, that goal might have been to have three months of living expenses set aside in a savings account, or maybe to pay off a credit card. But I had to accomplish *something* that justified the purchase. Thus, I used my desire for that material thing to move me closer to financial independence.

And that was not all.

3. *The purchase could be made only with cash and only when it did not interfere with savings or paying off debt.*

If it was going to impact either of those activities, then it was not yet time for me to reward myself with something that expensive.

So that's how I decided if I could afford something or not. If it had passed the "one-year wait test" *and* I could pay cash *and* buy it without any cutback to savings or paying off debts, then and only then could I afford it. If not, I had not earned it yet.

It has been instructive how few things I still had any interest in after one year, proving the purchase would have been both impulsive and wasteful, though it never feels that way at the time.

I remember a few years ago wanting a new pistol—badly. Having been a military marksman and later a civilian policeman, I am well trained and comfortable with firearms, and I feel my family is safer when I am armed. Years before I was out of debt, a new self-defense pistol was for sale, and I knew I would enjoy and use it for life. But, after my required one-year delay, I had lost my enthusiasm for it.

However, a smoker grill—which cost almost twice as much as the pistol—was still wanted after a year. So, I set a goal to save the required $1,100. I kept up with all my bills and my long-term financial goals, but, every time I got a little extra cash, I put it into an envelope. When I had saved the money, I bought the grill.

I am looking at it now through the window next to my desk. My family and our guests have enjoyed many years of pleasure around that grill, and not a dime I spent on it was missed or wasted. This is just one example of many, and, for several years now, as a result of this commonsense discipline, I have not made a single consumer purchase I regretted. Not one.

My circumstances now make this discipline unnecessary (which is, of course, the object of the exercise), but it is now my *habit* not to spend impulsively.

I can promise, if you will use this system, you will never buy anything you regret spending money on, and, over time, you will have thousands of dollars in your own bank account or working for you elsewhere that would otherwise have been gone from your hands forever. And, most important, you will be teaching yourself financial maturity.

So, the next time you want a new chair that costs two hundred dollars, first set a goal to put two hundred dollars into savings; afterward, save another two hundred dollars for the chair and buy it.

You might be thinking, "I'll never get anything if I follow that system!" To that, I reply, "You'll be free to get anything and everything *you have earned*—and without signing away your future to a creditor!"

And I don't care if it's on sale or not. If you can't pay cash for it, then you haven't earned it yet. Make up your mind that you will sit on empty orange crates before you make payments to a furniture company for a chair! Never add to your load of debt for comforts. Debt is sometimes unavoidable for necessities, but it is never—I repeat, *never*—necessary to use debt for comforts.

This does not mean you can never buy something expensive or use credit. As your circumstances improve, you can make exceptions. At the time of this writing, I just bought a very expensive automobile for my wife. And I financed it. I had the money to pay cash, but I got the loan at 5 percent interest. I used the cheap money, kept my cash in the bank, and set the term of the loan at eighteen months. But I know I can pay off the note at will. Years ago, had it been necessary to use credit to purchase transportation, I would not have bought such an expensive vehicle.

Here's another example. I soon intend to buy a Harley-Davidson motorcycle. I have wanted one for several years and could easily have bought one, but the expense has never met my own strict requirements. Every time the purchase met my own rules, I kept raising the bar, so to speak. I finally decided this would be my final self-imposed requirement: if I really want a Harley, I have to pay off a rental home I own, have a quality long-term tenant in place, have a cushion of a few months' rent in the rental account for unexpected upkeep expenses, and then use *the renters' money* to make the payment.

I have steadily refused to take my hard-earned income to make a motorcycle payment when it could be more wisely invested paying off a lifelong income-producing asset like a rental home.

That rental will soon be paid off. Then, I will buy the motorcycle and pay it off in two years with the renters' money—without using a dime of my own earned income. This has required that I wait several years to get it, even though I could have taken the cash out of the bank or easily made the payments. But I have now used my desire for an expensive motorcycle to move me forward, not backward, in my plan for financial independence.

And that brings me to another point: control your leisure expenses. Financing a new $20,000 boat because you like to fish—when you still owe for your home, your cars, and your credit card—is not a "healthy pastime that keeps me out of trouble." It's financial lunacy. Anyone determined to move forward and not backward must control his or her recreational spending.

My own splurge has always tended to be nice restaurants with my wife. But I can stop the expense at any time by simply not going out to eat. Find a way to relax that allows you to be in control of the expenses and stop them immediately if the need arises.

Quit Digging Yourself into a Hole

When I was in my early thirties, I was making about $60,000 a year, which was a lot more money then, than it is now, and, at the time, it was a lot of money to me. Some of my friends made a similar amount. Their attitude was, "Look at my income—and I am only in my early thirties! I can afford to live it up and get a few things I want. I'm trading in this Chevy for a Mercedes!"

But I didn't think like that. My thought was,

> *Look realistically at how little disposable income I have after taxes and expenses, even at $60,000 a year! And look at my total debt situation including the mortgage. I will never get free going farther down this path of stacking up payments. I have got to pay down debt! And, if my income improves, I won't get sloppy; I will pay my debts down faster! Who knows if these favorable business conditions will last forever?*

I absolutely refused to deceive myself into thinking that what went up could never come down. I made up my mind I was not about to live my entire life owing every payday to creditors, always just one missed check away from trouble.

A few poor decisions early in life can put you in a hole so deep, just getting back to even can take many years—years that should have been used to lay a foundation for real prosperity relative to your income with mental peace. A human lifespan is brief. Restraint early in life can help make it increasingly joyful, but it only takes but a few stupid decisions during those years to make it very difficult for a very long time.

MARGIN INSTEAD OF DEBT

When you are just starting out, income is low, many things are needed, and almost everything is wanted. Credit is commonly used as a way to bridge the gap. It has not always been that way.

Up until the 1960s, with the exception of a few years of easy credit preceding the infamous 1929 Wall Street Crash, most Americans disdained debt and avoided it. Savings were highly valued and considered something of great importance worth sacrificing for. The day they could "burn the mortgage" was a day of celebration toward which people consciously worked. In the 1960s, the only credit card commonly used was for one gas station—*maybe*—and it was paid off every month.

However, the explosion of credit card companies and easy credit terms in the 1970s proved irresistible to the middle class, not sophisticated enough to resist joining the artificial rise in living standards made possible by massive increases in personal debt.

Department stores issued their own credit cards. Homebuilders and automakers also profited from the public's acceptance of increasingly tenuous household balance sheets. To satisfy the demand, banks created new products with lower payments and lengthened payment schedules. Increasing levels of debt with longer contract terms became the new norm. Today, hardly a thing is sold in which some form of credit is not instantly available to anyone with a job. Fast-food chains now make an increasing portion of sales from credit cards.

Where has sanity gone?

About the same time personal debt was exploding upward, the government of the United States institutionalized "entitlements," which amounted to flagrant wealth confiscation and redistribution for votes; established foreign "aid," which is just plain giving away money; and, through a proliferation of agreements with various supranational organizations, committed its military to the role of global policeman, the expense of which has been the ruin of every former empire that has tried it. This produced rising budget deficits and the slow destruction of the value of the dollar. Over time, creeping inflation pushed the purchase price of a modest home from $15,000 to over $150,000—and much more than that in some areas.

Predictably, the total taxes collected from our paychecks, by all methods and all levels of government combined, went to levels that would make a feudal king blush. The squeeze play was on. The middle class began to experience stress fractures under the load of consumer debt, rising taxes, and falling dollar values—all of which intersect in our checkbooks, and only one of which we can directly stop.

Within just two decades, from the early 1960s to the early 1980s, most families found it necessary (not just a decision of personal preference) for both parents to pursue full-time careers. Two-income homes and latchkey children became the norm. Thirty years later, now in the second decade of a new century, two incomes are needed in most homes just to stay one step ahead of the wolf. What will things be like twenty years from now?

It is true you cannot do much about government spending and tax policy (though, if everyone called their representatives' offices instead of just sharing gripes with their friends, it would help a lot), but I have found if you take care of what you *can* control—such as your own level of debt—the things you can't control are much easier to manage.

An old saw says, "If a man could have half his wishes, he would double his trouble." Well, debt has allowed us to have half our wishes—and we have *more* than doubled our troubles. Debts chain you to the rat race. Debt is pulling us, like slaves, into the salt mines. And hardly any serious consideration is given to the possibility of avoiding consumer debt entirely. We end up grinding out our daily life in servitude to creditors, very often leading to serious problems in the home.

Are homes big enough to accommodate every need…pretty furnishings…impressive cars with the latest features…really worth it? They weren't to me. And, as I now have some of those things, I can tell you with even more conviction: *they are not.*

I heard on television recently that, in the year this paragraph is being written, the homes of more than one million families will be confronted with the risk of foreclosure. I suspect the joys of love and life are all but absent inside those homes. *And that is too high a price to pay for any material thing.*

I can do you no greater service than to awaken you to the potential miseries' debts chain to you. It is said that one hour of time well used in the morning is worth two at night. The same principle applies in life. Prudent decisions early in life produce exponential benefits in future years. So, if you would live well, you must act with greater wisdom than the lemming-like mass of debtors around you diving off the cliff.

As you cannot control inflation or taxes (beyond refusing to vote for anyone who promises one more dime of government aid to anyone for any reason), you must concentrate on the things you can control, the most important being your level of debt. In order to truly prosper, you will need a strong desire to be free of debt—a *passionate* desire, stronger than your appetite for more material possessions. Remember the first item on the list describing the new mindset you need in order to hang on to the slippery money that comes your way?

You create an emotional need to be financially independent.

So, as soon as possible, eliminate all credit card debt and have nothing but a modest house note and car payment. When you use extra money to pay down debt, two things happen that do not happen when you invest that money anywhere else:

1. There is no chance of losing your money.
2. You get a guaranteed compounding rate of return equal to whatever interest rate you were paying the

creditor. You can't get that deal with anything on Wall Street!

I know two men who are good examples of the different mindsets toward debt. These two men both work for me. One made over $100,000 last year; the other made about $50,000.

The more desperate of the two is the higher paid one. And *desperate* is the word. He has a nice car with a big payment and a big home on an interest-only "balloon" note. He and his wife certainly look prosperous, but I happen to know there is little comfort there.

The other employee isn't making but one-half as much. I have visited that man's apartment. The furnishings are modest but clean, and the apartment is attractive. His children are a delight, obviously loved, happy, and secure. He pays cash for functional used vehicles and is saving for a home. He is *never* desperate. The man in the apartment has my respect and admiration, and, frankly, he has the better life now—and, almost certainly, a brighter financial future.

The first man does not just spend to the limit but, worse, spends to the limit just servicing his accumulated debts. The wiser of the two lives with a mindset that says, "I will pay cash and keep a margin for the unexpected," and he does so on less than one-half the income.

> Whatever you have, spend less.
> —Samuel Johnson

The employee who lives within his means is relaxed when he calls me; the spendthrift is always nervous unless profits are flowing like a river. But life is cyclical. Highly profitable years come and then go, and lean years replace them for a season.

It is not good years or bad years that are normal—it is **changing conditions.** Happily, the higher-paid employee is coming around to a more sober assessment of the proper use of money.

MARGIN INSTEAD OF DEBT

Don't Be a Penny Pincher

People mentally shackled by greed are all about self and taking. They are black holes sucking everything in, and like the Dead Sea, give nothing out. Their insatiable needs become blindly self-inflicted miseries. But the responsible man or woman, the kind and judiciously generous man or woman will have outside forces rise to meet them on their path with gifts beyond their power to arrange.

In other words, *never withhold from others if you would live well yourself.* I am not recommending a pinched, miserly lifestyle. And please, never be a cheapskate. Freeloaders and scrooges are repugnant to everyone.

When a husband or father squeezes money so tightly he will never spend a little on his wife and children, or if he goes ballistic over minor expenditures, that man values money above his family, plain and simple. The justification, "I am just doing this for our own good," doesn't cut it. That kind of man is nothing but a nasty caricature of what a loving father and husband should be. A man who grasps every dollar and must approve personally of every expense and every purchase is a tyrant who has turned away from his family and made a god of money. No goal, including financial independence, is worth more than a family spirit of love and sharing. It is prudence I am recommending, not soul-pinching miserliness.

> No goal, including financial independence, is worth more than a family spirit of love and sharing.

As I've said before, I have always enjoyed nice restaurants, and I tip well in them. Even when we had much less money, I treated my young wife and me to good meals on the weekends, and I was generous with the tips. As soon as we could afford it (which was quite a few years into our marriage), we went on vacations. I was generous with my wife—within our means. We wore attractive clothes, but we did not buy anything on credit, and we avoided traps such as credit cards, expensive jewelry, high-end cars, furniture payments, and homes at the top of our price range. We have never borrowed a dime to go on a vacation or to purchase holiday gifts because, when necessary, we did without them.

Eventually, we had nice things—my wife drove a Jaguar and we purchased a wardrobe more than sufficient for all occasions—but we waited until it was appropriate. And we never made any of these purchases if they interfered with saving or giving.

We all need to go out to dinner or get some new clothes occasionally, or just stop for a splurge with the kids at an ice cream shop. What I am reproving is the middle-class norm of impulsive credit-card spending or accumulating debts for comforts and lifestyle.

And I have found that this debt-ridden lifestyle is not limited to the financially illiterate.

High Income Does Not Mean High Financial IQ

I recently had a conference with a wealth management advisor who works for my stock brokerage firm. Besides being a very bright gentleman, this man has a highly specialized education regarding how to handle money. After our consultation, in which we reviewed some of my affairs, I put a question to him:

> *Jay, you work for a top brokerage firm. Your clients are usually high-income earners a cut above the average guy on the street when it comes to money. You are an expensive asset for this firm to provide to their clients. I am sure someone with a small amount of funds invested does not often call for a consultation. Therefore, I assume you normally deal with the upper percentage of the general population in terms of wealth. I know for a fact that almost no one in the middle class*

handles their money properly. How often do the high-income clients you deal with handle their money well?

He said,

Almost never. If they have succeeded in business and make, say, $800,000 a year, they spend that $800,000 and borrow $800,000 more for lifestyle. Even the ones who may have several million invested have created a lifestyle that would consume that in a very few years. And they are constantly calling me wanting to know how soon they can retire!

> A farm is like a man—however great the income, if there is extravagance but little is left.
> —Cato the Elder

I am sometimes tempted to just tell them, "Never! It is not going to happen. It's your creditors who are going to retire early!"

No, I don't see financial restraint very often, no matter how high the income. The way you think is the exception. I wish I could get more of my clients to understand.

What is it I understand? How do I think? When you have finished reading this book and the others in the Common Sense for a Prosperous Life series, you'll know everything I know about these topics. I am holding nothing back, as you'll see in the next chapter in which I acknowledge that sometimes debt is necessary—and that we're not alone when facing our financial fears.

CHAPTER 4
THE PROPER USE OF CREDIT

*Make a decision that you are not staying where you are,
and you are not staying who you are.*

We all understand there are times when debt is the only option. If your car breaks down and you have no way to work, then your situation is going to get a lot worse if you don't borrow some money and buy a reliable car. You just have to work through those events.

Many people have accumulated debts simply by attempts to survive. If you are one of those, do not find fault with yourself. I know what it's like not to have enough money for the bills, to be desperately unhappy about it, and yet be at a loss for what to do to correct it. And no book and no person will have all the answers for every dilemma. Only God does. So, I am going to step over the line a little bit here and give a personal testimony.

When I was in that situation, someone brought to my wife's and my attention that the Bible said God wanted to help and that he was not a "get by" God, but a God of "more than enough." I still remember standing alone in my front yard pondering my impotence as a businessman and a money earner. It may sound humorous now, but, at the time, what I did next was totally sincere. I looked up and said,

> Lord, I have been told you want to help. So right now, I am giving you my life and my business. I am going to read the Bible and do everything it says to do to the best of my ability, so, if nothing gets better from here, it's your fault. And if you don't come through—I'm undone. Because I don't know what else to do!

I turned my life and my lack over to the only One not troubled by my weaknesses and deficiencies. My wife and I submerged ourselves in sermons and scriptures that gave us hope. Things didn't change as fast as I wanted, but things did begin to get better.

The Importance of Reading, Prayer, and Active Faith

When I was very young, the first really wealthy man I ever met told me, "Mark, the difference in where you are now and where you will be ten years from now will be decided by the books you read and the people you associate with."

That made sense to me, and I knew I wanted out of the hand-to-mouth life. Plus, I had enough sense to know that, if he made every week what I made in a year, one of us needed to change. So, I decided to read a self-help book for at least fifteen minutes a day, and, for the next seven years, I kept that commitment, though I detested reading.

While reading, I watched the clock constantly, anxious for the fifteen minutes to pass. For seven years I stuck with it, but I got absolutely nothing out of it. I might as well have been reading the phone book.

Then, inexplicably, after seven years, some switch in my brain finally clicked, and I became a voracious reader with good retention of the subject matter. I eventually had to force myself to cut back on my reading, and, to this day, I am never willingly without something instructive to read close at hand.

If you want to know how you can move ahead in life, consider well these next two sentences:

> *Winners do consistently what losers will only do occasionally.*
>
> *Winners want it badly enough to do something about it—whether they like it or not.*

If you are a person of faith, it might be wise to highlight the scriptures of your faith that have to do with provision and guidance and blessing and *read them aloud to yourself every day*. Then make a decision that you are not staying **where** you are, and you are not staying **who** you are. Lift your life to God and say, as I did,

> *God, I believe you exist, and you are always a good and abundant God. I accept it on faith that you hear me now and you have made a place for me in your good plans. No loving father would want to see his child poor and unhappy. I am willing to do whatever I know to do to improve my life, but I know I will need help.*
>
> *Please show me the way to a more satisfying life. Christ said, in so many words, that those who look to you in their need would see God's supply and direction opened to them. "God blesses those who are poor and realize their need for him, for the Kingdom of Heaven is theirs." —Matthew 5:3, New Living Translation, NLT*
>
> *Each day I am going to do the little or the much I can see to do that day, and I am going to look to you to do the rest. Give me eyes to see what I am to do next and I will step out in faith. It is recorded that you fed thousands of people with only a couple of fish and a few pieces of bread. If that is true,*

THE PROPER USE OF CREDIT

then the fact that I am not exactly brimming over with ideas and talents will be no problem for you. I am putting you "in business" to do as you see fit with me. And, if you will teach me how to prosper, I will bless others.

For those of you in discouraging circumstances right now, let me share this: a man named George Shinn once related his encouraging life story to an audience, and in that audience was one very discouraged young man—me. He was the youngest recipient ever to receive the Horatio Alger Award, an award given in recognition of exceptional achievement in business. Horatio Alger's books featuring young heroes of industry and character inspired an earlier generation of Americans to reach for their dreams.

When George was a young man, his fledgling business was on the verge of bankruptcy. He spent his last $500 seeking professional counsel from a firm in Atlanta. After they reviewed his situation, they told him his business had no chance to survive. George had spent his last $500 for professional help, only to be told he was going to fail. He was devastated. The senior partner of the firm, in a show of compassion, walked him to the elevator. Just before George stepped into the elevator, the gentleman put his arm around George's shoulder and said kindly, "George, I'm so sorry, but you don't have a prayer."

As George was driving along Interstate 85 heading back to South Carolina, he began to cry so violently, he had to pull over. The wrenching finality of the words, "George, you don't have a prayer," kept rolling through his mind. Then, in that darkest of moments, God broke through. George suddenly realized that a prayer was the only thing he *did* have left.

On the side of the interstate, in a flood of desperate tears, George asked God into his life and promised that, if he were allowed to prosper, he would never fail to tell the story of where his business success came from. George did prosper, and he has kept that promise.

But it should also be noted that George went to work with a renewed vigor and overcame many obstacles. Did you notice in that story just how desperately George Shinn wanted to succeed? The will to rise must be made of stern stuff! Reading and prayer are essential, but so is an *active* faith.

Faith Without Works Is Dead

Prayer is not a cure-all for the lazy. In business, it is guidance for the active. You have to be doing something for God to bless. You can pray all you want, but, if you aren't doing anything but working by the hour and then going home to watch television, there is little for God to do.

It is foolish to expect God to drive a parked car. You must be *doing something*. Now, I am not suggesting you act impetuously or rashly, but you have to be open to an intuitive lead or an opportunity. If someone offers you a good chance, you have to take it—then learn how to succeed at it afterward.

Answers to prayers are often like bumper cars at a carnival. If you are diligent and moving, God can bump you in the right direction. As you keep pressing and trying, God keeps bumping you—sometimes through great trials—until you are moving in the right direction. It isn't very pleasant at the time, but it is often the way prayers are answered.

Things may not change as quickly or as much as we wish because *it is our character more than our checkbook that God wishes to develop*. God can put money in your bank account, but strengthening your character takes time and some pressure. More success or money than a person can properly handle is not a "good and perfect gift." —James 1:17, New International Version

> Lord, give me nothing before I am ready for it.

I constantly pray, "Lord, give me nothing before I am ready for it." And I am wise enough at my age to mean it. Twenty years ago, I thought I was ready for it all. Looking back, he gave me as much as I could handle without becoming obnoxious.

I must confess I am dismayed when I hear so many sermons expounding that God wants us to prosper, without the exhorters ever mentioning that the listener had better be doing something that at least has the potential to be profitable. Usually, the pitch is that God wants to bless you as soon as you prove your sincerity by sending *them* some money, which, it is implied, proves to God that you are stepping out in faith on his promises.

Look, I am all in favor of intelligently considered and cheerful giving, but, if you want to see an increase in your finances, you had better be a little more sophisticated than that. Let me say this clearly:

It isn't sending someone a check that proves your faith; it is the determination in your heart to refuse to accept staying where you are now.

And that doesn't cost you a dime.

Doing something for yourself that can lead to profits or becoming a valuable member of an income-producing enterprise. *That's* what will make a difference to your finances. To make an ongoing income, one must build something, buy something, or be a part of something that makes profits.

Know this: God is not sending money to your house in exchange for your last donation to a television personality while you do little more than wait for it. God is not some dimwitted cosmic genie who gives you hundreds for tens. Faith requires *work*. Faith and work are Siamese twins. When one is missing the other isn't there, because each always brings the other one with it.

When it comes to finances, you must realize prayer and charity are ineffective unless you are making every sincere and intelligent effort you can to help yourself. And intelligent efforts include the time you use to improve yourself—reading my books is an example—and being mentally open for a workable opportunity. Don't feel pressured to act rashly.

Now, understanding the importance of a foundation of prayer, faith, and sustained work to improve our self, leading to acting on inspired ideas or visible opportunity, we can also begin to better understand the proper use of credit.

Thoughts on Debt

My argument against consumer debt should not be construed as prohibiting all borrowing. Not all debt is inappropriate. Debt is a necessary and useful tool to build wealth or provide a home, one that is modest relative to income, which would be out of reach on a cash basis. But *debt for lifestyle is out.* Credit purchases of vacations, furniture, jewelry, clothing, holiday gifts, and restaurant meals are strictly off-limits. They make great rewards as you earn them, but they are *never* credit purchases.

My stepfather, Frank Echols, was always buying something new. A new truck…a new motor home…just anything. He chided me once for being too conservative. I told him, "Frank, I don't want to look rich. I want my freedom." When freedom—*financial independence*—is the goal, instead of just having more things, the way you handle your money is totally different.

> Let all the learned say what they can, 'Tis ready money makes the man.
> —William Somerville

I read that Einstein marveled at the stupendous power of compounding interest. Anyone who has seen a chart of what money can do as interest compounds will understand why even Einstein would be amazed by the potency of this tool. Well, personal debt puts that stupendous power to work *against you* instead of *for you.*

THE PROPER USE OF CREDIT

So, I say again: if you have debt, eliminate it as soon as possible. Extra money paid against debt is never in danger of being lost, and it gives you an immediate guaranteed return. For all but the most financially savvy, paying down debt is the best investment you can make.

If you do feel you have that kind of savvy and are capable of earning a greater return on your capital than paying off your debts will accomplish, then go for it. Just don't bet the farm. A talented person taking a calculated risk is something to be encouraged, even if things don't work out. The younger you are at the time, the better. And you might still want to hedge your bet.

I have taken a big swing once or twice—and lost. I lost some sleep over it, but I recovered because I have never put myself in a position to be wiped out.

Here is my simple wisdom on debt condensed into a few sentences:

> *Some type of debt is constantly being sold to us as the way to get ahead. It is, in fact, the way to never get ahead. Consumer debt is "living on money you ain't made yet." And that is presuming an awful lot. Life is full of the unexpected, much of it good, and some of it is not good at all. Ready money will fix most of it. So lay a strong foundation before you spend.*

Consider this before you assume the slightest debt:

Money is the lifeblood of every home and every business, and it takes much more "ready money" to be ready than you think.

Guidelines for Borrowing

The wise use of credit is intended to be beneficial to the long-term prosperity of a nation and its responsible citizens. As I said earlier, more than once, it is *lifestyle debt* that is the killer. So, after spending years with every thought bent toward getting out of debt, and then finally seeing my dream of being totally debt-free come to pass, I signed papers for a large line of credit. But this line of credit will only be used to act on opportunity, never for foolish consumption.

The proper use of credit will fund business or investment, thus creating wealth when your skills are ready for it. Unfortunately, most people view credit upside down: as the way to get things they haven't yet earned. They ignore the responsible use of borrowed money and instead tie up the credit available to them acquiring unearned lifestyle rewards.

Credit may help you get the things you want before you can actually pay for them, but, as you may soon discover for yourself, you will not be richer for it; you will actually just be getting older and falling farther behind on the wealth curve.

Not surprisingly, using debt properly requires prudent precautions. Having a line of credit does not mean you have to run out and use it. I have strict guidelines to provide two layers of protection for my borrowing decisions:

1. It is said, once every thousand years a black swan is born. For investors, a "black swan" refers to an external event that cannot be anticipated, such as the September 11, 2001, terrorist attacks, the credit/housing meltdown in 2008, and the global virus pandemic that shut down the world's economies in 2020. A shrewd investor will have a plan to survive the appearance of a black swan.

    So, my first rule is this: **I will not borrow, even to make money, if I do not have enough free cash set**

THE PROPER USE OF CREDIT

aside to cover the note on the loan for one year. During the first year of the loan, I will set aside enough funds to cover the note for the next year. I want always to have one year of safety built-in, in case circumstances suddenly change for the worse. This is my protection against a black swan.

2. **I will not borrow to the point that the amount of debt I assume affects my peace of mind.** *If anything you do interferes with sleep, then you have overreached.* You will no longer have the capacity to wait calmly for events to unfold in your favor. For me, this means **I will not borrow more than I am able to pay out of my own pocket if it becomes necessary.**

I do understand there are creative methods of financing to use when conducting business. My point is not that I will not avail myself of them, but that I will not be put into a position where something can go wrong and take me down with it. I will have the ready money to cover the obligations I assume, even if things don't go the way I planned.

*Never put on shoes that are too tight
when you are borrowing money.*

Now I realize these are some pretty tight standards for borrowing. Not every person who reads this book will need to follow such strict limits on debt for business purposes. But I share my own rules to give you food for thought before you use credit, even for productive purposes. Confucius wisely wrote, "The cautious seldom err."

As you reach for greater wealth, especially if borrowed money is involved, you have to stay balanced. You must not overreach and jeopardize everything you have gained thus far. Every transaction has a potential downside. You are making a correct decision only if your means will allow you to ride that downside out. Not even Lehman Brothers, formerly one of the world's largest brokerage firms, was big enough to violate this rule and survive.

A man visited me recently to ask for my advice. He had leased a building to expand his business, and his partner had skipped out on him. This left him solely responsible for the lease, and his business had not grown as he anticipated. Now he is stuck with the entire lease payment and is behind on his own home mortgage. The loss of his house is not far away, with several children, he's worried for their future…and he has a mighty unhappy wife. Unfortunately, I had no advice to give him. The outcome was no longer in his hands.

He was eagerly ambitious but imprudent. He let his reach exceed his ability to grasp. That is easy to do with credit. Learn from him and from me:

- Have a margin for safety in everything you do, but particularly when borrowing money.
- Do not put yourself in the position in which you are on the hook if other people fail to keep their promises.
- Do not put yourself in the position in which you will lose everything you have gained to date if something goes wrong.
- Be willing to wait for a better plan.
- When it comes to business deals—especially when debt is involved—never test the depth of the water with both feet. Meaning, never fully commit without a backup plan.

Since this was written, I have learned this man has lost his business, his home, and—even more regrettably—his family.

THE PROPER USE OF CREDIT

There *is* a proper use of credit, and it begins with a lesson this man had, sadly, not yet learned: have a plan in place to work through unexpected difficulties before you do anything with borrowed money.

CHAPTER 5
PROGRESS REQUIRES A WRITTEN PLAN

The road from struggle to comfort is measured in years; anything under a decade is remarkable.

If you stick your finger into a glass of water and lift it out, a few drops of water will drip from the end of your finger. If those drops fall into an empty cup, they will barely wet the bottom. But that same small act, if you persist, will eventually fill the cup, and then the very next drop that falls from your fingertip will cause the cup to *overflow*.

That is a good analogy for how to handle money. The drops represent dollars, and the cup represents a written plan that captures those dollars, so they do not slip away. Without a written plan to secure the dollars you earn, they *will* get away from you.

But there is an obvious problem. In the beginning, the drops seem to be too few to matter, and the cup will seem too big ever to be filled. And it is our nature to be impatient, to want shortcuts. We read about others getting rich quickly, and we want to find out how we can do it just as effortlessly.

PROGRESS REQUIRES A WRITTEN PLAN

That's why books about "how I made millions trading stocks" and "how to become rich in real estate" sell so well.

I am not opposed to such books; I have read a few of them myself. But no matter what you do to increase your income, do not fool yourself and do not let yourself be fooled. The truth is it is going to take years for you to become proficient and successful at anything. The road from struggle to comfort is measured in years; anything under a decade is remarkable.

True, on rare occasions someone comes into riches in a short period of time, but, when that is the case, the character and maturity necessary to handle the new circumstances are often lacking. (Pick up any tabloid for details of the most recent examples.) So, no matter what you do for a living, anyone who wishes to earn and retain a comfortable position in life must first master the fundamentals of money—or they will not keep that money for long.

Learning the Fundamentals

I had a conversation once with the owner of the karate studio where my daughters had taken lessons. He had a son and daughter who were both karate black belts. He mentioned they also both played the piano. Just by way of making conversation, I asked him how they were at it. He said they both had approximately equal talent, but his daughter was a much better pianist. I asked him why.

He said,

> My son will open a lesson book and turn to the last page, which has the most difficult piece of music to play. He figures that if he can play that piece well then he doesn't need to know what is on all the pages before it, and he will practice until he has perfected that piece.

But my daughter will open at the first page and practice every successive lesson—whether she thinks she already knows it or not—until she has mastered it.

They are both talented, and both have equal amounts of persistence, but she passed him a long time ago. Playing one piece of difficult music well is no substitute for mastering the fundamentals first.

The parallel to the point I am making is obvious. Talent alone is not enough; neither is greater income or more education. These things may give us more options to choose from, but they will not change the direction of our choices. Clear thinking on the major issues of life and a strongly held commitment to building our life on a solid foundation *will* change our choices and our outcome. Supplying that universal need is why these books were written. Robert Kiyosaki points out in his *Rich Dad* books that the rich have a plan for their money before it is earned. I was not surprised when I read that. I had been using a series of simple financial plans many years before his books were written, and I can tell you there is no way to endorse sufficiently the difference that following a written plan makes.

A clear plan for how you will allocate and use the money that comes to you is a requirement for anyone who intends to become financially independent. There is no such thing the world over as a self-made man or woman who went from lack to wealth with no plan for how they would use the money that came under their control.

Emotional Investment

It is, however, of little help to write down wishes and call them goals. This is not how to use a written plan. All genuine

PROGRESS REQUIRES A WRITTEN PLAN

motivation originates in the emotional/spiritual portions of our being. Logic will not produce sustained actions.

The truth is unless we are emotionally invested, when we look at our goals' list, our mind will quickly begin to wander to the business of the day and we might as well be looking at a blank sheet of paper (that will happen some anyway). So, how do we make written goals become spiritually and emotionally compelling? How do we bridge the gap from what is logically desirable to a genuine enthusiasm?

Here is what I do:

I write out every day, by hand, my immediate goals.

As I write, I have a prayerful mental posture, as if asking for guidance to get there, though I may not pray consciously at all. I may, in quiet thought, ask God not to let my life be wasted pursuing the wrong things or pursuing the right things for the wrong reasons. I often ask that He give me nothing before I am ready for it. This cleans away ego, coveting, and pride, which corrupt worthy objectives.

If it is a material thing, I may look at pictures I have saved that reinforce my emotional connection through visual imagery.

If you want bigger responsibilities with more pay at work, you might look at photographs of successful men or women engaged in business and imagine yourself gaining influence. Remind yourself to be looking for ways you can improve your department or your relationships with other workers. Be watchful for anything you can do that can create greater efficiencies for others one level below or above you.

My oldest daughter Scarlett just began her career. Before she left for her first day on the job, I told her this true story.

Scarlett, years ago I read a book written in the early 1900's that was a collection of interviews with men and women of great accomplishment. These talented men and women were explaining how they made their lives so productive. Let me share with you one of the stories that might be particularly helpful for you to hear now.

A company that was one of the early oil and gas producers in Texas hired a young man to help the many assistants to the executive staff with their clerical duties. His job required him to work on the same floor as the company owner and top executives. One evening, about half an hour after everyone else had left for the day, the owner came out of his office and saw this man still sitting at his desk. He asked him, "Didn't they tell you that quitting time was five o'clock?" The new employee said, "Yes, they did. But I did not understand it to mean that I had to leave at five." "Well, what are doing here?" the owner inquired. "I saw that you were still in your office and I stayed behind in the event that I might be of some service to you," he answered. "Well, get me a pencil then," said the owner.

That man, being interviewed because his life had become so successful, related that the owner at the first place he worked got into the habit of looking for him first when he needed something, and he eventually became one of the top owner/executives in the oil and gas business himself. Scarlett, to prosper at work make yourself indispensable to someone that matters.

I am proud to report that she did.

That should be an instructive aside for anyone starting out in active life. Make yourself absolutely necessary.

Now, let's resume the discussion of setting goals.

If I am seeking money, truthfully, like any of us, my first thought is about the list of expenditures I set for each year and getting that list done. But then, I also often think of the organizations or individuals my wife and I have helped in

PROGRESS REQUIRES A WRITTEN PLAN

the past year, and that there is more to do. I like to think in specific terms of someone that really deserves to receive an act of kindness and generosity. This builds my faith because I know for a fact that responsible and generous motives move things in the invisible world of the spirit.

If tension creeps in, such as the natural thought, "How can I do any of this?" I remind myself that I do not have to answer that question. I am only confirming what I want my life to be about and asking for guidance. I only need to look for what can be done *today*. I remind myself that I too will need to receive surprising acts of divine generosity: a flash of inspired thought or the right person appearing with the talents I need to get to the next level. I don't have to figure it all out.

> A branch connected to the vine does not strain to bud; it is effortless. Budding is simply the result of staying connected.

I may mentally reflect on scriptures such as John 15:5: "I am the vine, you are the branches. He who abides in Me, and I in him, bears much fruit; for without Me you can do nothing." (New King James Version [NKJV]) I am willing. He is able. I am the vine. He is the branch. A branch connected to the vine does not strain to bud; it is effortless. Budding is simply the result of staying connected.

However, some mornings, if I am not in the mood, or too busy, I will skip the whole goal process altogether. It is not to become a chore. So, as you do this, day after day, seek to make it a pleasant time. Write each goal anew that is important to you in the current season of your life, feel it anew, maybe look at images of it, pray anew, and do this until that goal has an emotional attachment within you.

Do this almost daily, but do not be concerned with how you might accomplish or arrange the things you are envisioning. Trust that the way will be presented. Just build a bridge from a purely logical desire that lacks internal power to an emotional/spiritual purpose that becomes a true goal—a goal that feels good and one you are emotionally connected to.

These goals usually begin with material needs—and that is perfectly fine—but, over the course of your life, you will find they will become more and more about giving your life away: "…whoever loses his life for My sake will find it." —Matthew 16:25b, NKJV

Your Plan

Your plan should be simple, and it should grow and change with you over the years. But, if you intend eventually to live free of financial stress, you must decide ahead of time what you will do with the money that comes to you.

Write down, in the order you intend to do it, what the next money you earn will be committed to accomplishing. And don't let the term "financial plan" scare you off, suggesting thoughts of complicated formulas. Those things are only for the rich.

In the rest of this book, I will show you the financial plans that have brought me, one by one, to where I am now. They couldn't be simpler. In fact, my first financial plan was…only one step.

CHAPTER 6
FINANCIAL PLAN 1

What do rich people do that evidently no one in my family has ever known to do?

I was twenty-four when I wrote down my first financial plan. As I made a new habit of each objective, I gradually added steps to my plan. My goal was financial independence, and I was constantly asking myself, "What should I do next? What is the next most logical step?"

We will look at those successive choices as this book continues. However, right now, check out my first plan, and you will see my first step toward wealth was a decision to begin the habit of giving away money. That fact is so contradictory to logic, it requires an explanation.

Financial Plan 1

1. Honor the law of the tithe. Invite God into your affairs. Give 10 percent of your net income to your house of worship, or if you do not attend a house of worship, to organizations that help others less fortunate. Live on the 90 percent that is left.

Should You Read This?

I realize people of different religious faiths or of no religious inclination at all may one day read what I am writing. And, if I may add a bit of honest humor, as I wrote this on faith and had no idea if it would ever be purchased and read by anyone, it is also possible very few will ever read what I am writing.

I do not wish to press my personal religious beliefs upon anyone. Sincerely, I don't. I have wrestled with whether I should exclude even the least discussion of tithing from all my writings on how to handle money. I knew that if I approached the subject at all I might seem to be preaching an unsolicited sermon. And I did not want to write a book directed to members of any particular faith since common-sense rules for the proper handling of capital have no such limitations.

Finally, I concluded there was simply no way around it because giving away 10 percent of my income was the first long-term financial decision I ever made. I gave it a higher priority even than saving. Such a paradox deserves a thorough explanation.

> Every millionaire I met suggested I seriously consider the importance of a lifestyle of giving in order to facilitate my own well-being.

So, though it is decidedly not my intention to proselytize for my particular faith, I include these thoughts because, in my opinion, I cannot skip this subject without doing a great injustice to you, the reader.

Now, you can consider my reasoning and then accept or dismiss this portion of my writings. Or you can skip this section completely. Your choice. But I think this discussion of giving and charity is one of the most important if you wish to become wealthier in money and happiness.

So, please, stay with me through the next pages. You will be introduced to some important life-building information which I consider an integral part of the nuts and bolts of money, business, and life choices.

FINANCIAL PLAN 1

An Explanation of the Tithe Principle

Why on earth was my first step toward creating greater prosperity...to give away 10 percent of my income?

I mentioned earlier that when I was quite young, I met my first very wealthy man. Within a couple of years, I had been introduced to several other millionaires. I never knew them well, but I guess they saw my sincerity and wanted to pass along a little of what they thought might help me. Along with the normal advice—work for myself and read carefully selected books to prepare myself for larger responsibilities—every one of them eventually suggested I seriously consider the importance of a lifestyle of giving in order to facilitate my own well-being.

Did their suggestion—of giving away money to prepare a path to my own wealth—strike me as strange? I can tell you honestly that, having come from a background so removed from any conversations about money or ambition, I knew so little about what millionaires might think that *nothing* they said struck me as strange. I had no preconceived notions at all. I was just curious and wanted to know how they had become wealthy.

Perhaps because I was so young, they apparently took no offense when I just plain asked them, "What do rich people do that evidently, no one in my family has ever known to do?" And each and every one of the wealthy persons I met mentioned *tithing* somewhere in that conversation.

The word *tithe* means "a tenth." These men explained to me that, according to the Bible (and perhaps many other religious writings), the first tenth of what we earn belongs to God. God explains through scripture that the first 10 percent of your increase is His, and, when you bring Him that part which he reserves for Himself, there are blessings and benefits. And, if you *keep* that part which is His for your own use, there are penalties.

So tithing means returning the *first* 10 percent of each dollar you earn back to God. Why the first? Because making it the first thing we do with our money will require our faith. We then look to God to meet our needs with the 90 percent that is left. The tithe points us *first* to God to meet our needs rather than to our money. And, God cannot accept being second. God is first - in everything. That is the preeminence of God, and first is a position He will not relinquish to anyone or anything. He is worthy of more than a little bit of the leftovers if all the bills are paid.

God's view, as it was related to me, is that all we earn comes from Him, either in opportunities placed on our life path or from the talents He gifted us with. Indeed, he has given us our very lives. As an act of worship, we bring the first 10 percent of all our increase to Him in gratitude and acknowledge Him as the source of our supply.

> The tithe is to protect and bless us.

In this act, we also demonstrate that we can be trusted with greater material riches. The tithe is then used to supply the means to minister to the spiritual and physical needs of others, but supporting God's work is not the purpose of our tithe. The tithe is our acknowledgement that He is the source of all we have been given and that we can be trusted to return the portion that He says is His alone. He then promises to protect us in our difficulties and increase us.

It is God's way of protecting us from the human weakness of looking to money alone for our security and welfare, a condition of the heart the Bible calls "the love of money." What could be more fraught with dangers than a creature that does not own a single breath of his life deciding he does not need God if he can accumulate enough money? The tithe is to protect and bless *us*.

We are free to conduct our business with the 90 percent that is left. In this act of returning *His part* of our earnings we prove our own willingness to rely upon God's financial system, trusting He is willing and able to take care of us and increase us.

He then promises to bless and *increase* the 90 percent we keep. Thus, we are promised, the 90 percent with God's blessing resting upon it will eventually bring more abundance and peace into our lives than the entire 100 percent would have, had we kept it all for our own use.

The tithe proves our willingness to *begin* to transfer our trust from our little store of money to the God that created human commerce. It is not an end step of great maturity and sacrifice; it is the beginning of two walking together on a journey where, formerly, one walked alone.

> Tithing is not some ancient religious ritual.

In the Old Testament of the Bible, Abraham is recorded as the first man to enter a covenant with God and is considered the father of the Arabic and Hebrew peoples. He paid tithes hundreds of years before tithing was commanded in the law of God.

Jesus reconfirmed the tithe during his earthly ministry, recorded in Luke 11:42. And elsewhere in the New Testament in 2 Corinthians 9:6, after the requirements of the Judaic laws were replaced with grace—grace being right standing with God apart from fulfilling Old Testament laws such as tithing—systematic giving is taught again.

In other words, tithing is not some ancient religious ritual. In the Bible, tithing was to be a permanent part of all human affairs—before the law was established, during the law, and after the law was fulfilled in Christ and replaced with grace. Within 2 Corinthians 9:8, it reveals that as man does what God requires—with a willing heart—God promises His partnership with us.

And So, I Started

If I had heard of tithing before my discussions with these men, I do not remember it. I knew, of course, that people gave money to their places of worship or the buildings couldn't have been there. I understood nothing, however, about the principle of reciprocity, of sowing and reaping: the view that your life unfolds *over time* in response and in proportion to your own chosen actions, that liberal giving begets liberal living.

The Bible promises each person will reap what they sow—later than they sow and in more abundance than they sow just like any other planted crop—*but not necessarily where they sow.* The men who introduced me to this principle claimed it had been a powerful force for their own good, and, by so doing, they planted a seed in my mind that began to germinate.

> Tithing would prove to be one of the most beneficial decisions I could make.

I started tithing a few years later when I was a twenty-four-year-old policeman. At the time, my take-home pay was $175 a week. I was not attending a church, and I was not particularly religious. But I had never forgotten what I had been told about tithing, and, realizing I had no training other than that of being a policeman, I knew if I were ever going to find my way to a larger place in the world, I certainly could use some divine help. So, it just seemed to me that tithing was the right first step.

And, to be quite truthful, I was so broke and so completely devoid of any way forward, I knew of nothing else within my power to do. But this is also true: I felt even then that, as my life unfolded in future years, tithing would prove to be one of the most beneficial decisions I could make. In fact, I somehow knew it, so I made it my first sincere step toward changing my future.

# FINANCIAL PLAN 1

Why? Because, even though in my line of work I was around the worst examples of humanity, and even though I was not concerned about spiritual matters at that time in my life, *I believed that God existed and that He would keep His word to anyone that trusted Him.*

And a decision to tithe or not is always just that simple. It was, in my mind, a child's equation: if I do A, God does B. If God may or may not do B, why do A?

I did not make up the equation. It was offered to me, as it is offered to everyone. The question we all must answer for ourselves is, "Does the God making the offer really exist? Can He be trusted?"

Frankly, I had little to decide between. On $175 a week, and no skill but driving a police car, I wasn't getting out unless God helped me. And if He didn't? Well, when you are that broke and someone tells you there's a door open, you may debate it for a while, but you are eventually going through it if you really want out.

I had been blessed with good health, a job I loved, a good mind, and a great family—things a lot of the people I came into contact with as a policeman did not have—and it just seemed appropriate to me that I show my gratitude. Plus, if it is not too impudent to admit it, I wanted some help to add financial comfort to my list of blessings. And there was precious little hope of that in my line of work at the time.

I can clearly remember debating whether I could afford to give away 10 percent of my income—that $70 a month was huge to me at the time. I was barely making it on my pay as a policeman and it seemed seriously doubtful that I could get by on even that much less. But I was desperate for a better life financially, and I knew I needed to do something.

I wanted to change the course of my life, and I did not know what else to do to bring that change about. Even though I felt fulfilled by being in law enforcement, I did not want a pedestrian and common life. Growing up I'd seen firsthand what it was like to live in a home where finances were a struggle, and I did not want that repeated in my home. Though I was not married at the time, I wanted a better life for my future family than I could provide as a policeman.

I no longer remember all the back and forth I went through mentally—I'm sure there was a good bit of it—but, at some point, I made the plunge and gave away 10 percent of my next paycheck. Ever since, tithing has been a part of my budget just like any other obligation.

For better or worse, in my mind I walked irreversibly through the door. Even today, I am the only person I have ever heard of who started tithing before I started attending a church! And, to my knowledge, I have never missed tithing on a single earned dollar.

In other words, I started doing it God's way, as I understood it. And, for the next thirty-plus years, up to the time I am writing these words, my comfort and wealth have increased.

There never seemed to be anything supernatural about it, but my income climbed. At first, it was just a little each year, but the little became larger. Eventually, some single-year jumps in income were over $100,000.

I can also recall several instances when huge potential reversals never materialized, as if I had divine protection—which I believe I did. In those instances, I often thought of Psalm 41:1–3 (NKJV):

Blessed is he who considers the poor;
The Lord will deliver him in time of trouble.
The Lord will preserve him and keep him alive,
And he will be blessed on the earth;
You will not deliver him to the will of his enemies.
The LORD will strengthen him on his bed of illness;
You will sustain him on his sickbed.

FINANCIAL PLAN 1

Not a Trick

I believe the beneficial effects of giving will work for everyone, just as kindness produces a certain response from life no matter who gives it. Systematic giving or the absence of it—I now believe, just as did the wealthy men I spoke with so many years ago—will have an impact on your life, for better or for worse. It is our choice whether the law works for or against us, but the law will not be suspended for anyone.

When someone with money problems comes to me for counseling, I begin by asking,

> *Do you tithe? Have you given God the right to enter into your financial affairs? Is tithing a part of your budget or have all your spending choices left God out of your business matters and made tithing "impossible"?*
>
> *Have you given him what is his, or have you for your entire life taken every dime you could earn and used it all on yourself?*

The usual response is, "No. I just can't afford to." Then I ask one more question: "Before you got into this jam, were you a committed tither?" You can guess the answer for yourself.

Systematic giving, I believe, causes unseen forces to come to our aid, either inside us—in thoughts that are wealth seeds—or in outer circumstances—through serendipitous relationships and/or events.

However, if the giving is done on a quid pro quo basis just to see what you can get out of it and how quickly, the generous power of the principle is violated, and the fruit will not ripen to harvest. But, if you give out of gratitude and obedience, you are planting seeds for a *future* harvest. *It will not show up next week.* Seeds need time to grow, but interest *is* compounding its way into your future. Just remember, God didn't say, "Do whatever you feel is right." He said, "The first ten percent is mine."

Tithing is not a trick we play on God to indebt him to us. Tithing is not a cosmic gimmick to "check it out and see if it works." It is a decision to begin a partnership lifestyle. It is the *first* allocation from the *top* of every net dollar.

Now, I have heard preachers assert that the tithe should be taken from the gross income. However, unless you feel an internal dictate to do that, I respectfully disagree. How can I be held responsible for money that is not mine and will never be under my control? Taxes belong to the government. They are never mine, and, if you have any doubts, ask your country's tax authority and they will clear that point up for you quickly.

I have tithed on my gross income many times, but from gratitude and never from duty. Although neither point of view—gross or net—can be proven categorically from any scripture of which I am aware, I believe my point of view to be the most congruent with common sense where scripture is not clear.

The Bottom Line of Why I Tithe

A story is told of a farmer about to go bust because of a drought. He told God, if God would send rain, from that day forward the farmer would give back to God 10 percent of whatever he earned. Later, when he had become wealthy, he was asked if he really thought his giving had anything to do with the reversing of his circumstances. He said, "I don't know. But I'd be afraid to stop."

Well, I feel the same way. I think tithing had a lot to do with my protections and improving circumstances over the years, though I can't prove it.

But I would not stop, even if I were suddenly made aware that my assumption was completely false.

FINANCIAL PLAN 1

Why not? Because I know how beneficial cheerful and consistent giving has been for *me* when I see what my dollars are doing for others who cannot help themselves. Their situation, but for the grace of God, could have been my own.

God loves you and God loves me. Not because we are lovable but because that is His nature. He desires a relationship. He is always seeking a way into our lives, and how we connect with Him is through our trust in Him, not our performance. A simple decision to believe He exists and has goodwill and love for us, and to trust Him, is how we invite him in.

One of the areas in which He seeks a relationship is in our finances. Why our money? Well, He is interested in our welfare. We need money and He knows it. In such a critical part of our life, we need Him to be active, and He knows that better than we do. He ordained human economic activity and He knows more about finances than you or I ever will.

Scriptures explain that, when a man or a woman commits himself or herself to tithe, they activate a covenant—a legally valid promise of intent—between God and man. In the tithe covenant, man agrees to give (or more accurately, faithfully return God's portion to him), and God promises to meet that act of faith and obedience with increased blessing.

Now, I'm no theologian; if you are, you can undoubtedly parse it out more accurately for yourself. I'm just trying to explain it well enough that you, the reader, can understand why I decided to put the principle to work for me instead of *against me*.

As a Christian, I believe in a personal God who provided instructions for abundant living in a collection of writings called the Bible. And, as money is a vital life issue, many of those instructions from God to man concern a man's use of his money. For the sake of clarity, I am going to relate some of those scriptures, but, again, I am not proselytizing for my faith. I am only explaining why my own logic led me to conclude that tithing was an important principle in the proper handling of capital.

If you are of a different faith, then you may find parallels within the teachings of your own religion. If you are of no religious conviction at all, you may want to read this out of curiosity because I put it to the test when I was *broke*. Nothing in the more than thirty intervening years has given me any reason to believe I acted foolishly.

God is not opposed to someone accumulating money. The Bible is explicit that the wealthiest men in scripture were made that way through their relationships with God. What He opposes is our making an *idol* of money, that is, letting the money become our trust and confidence. Be aware: the transfer of what we trust in for our welfare, from the living God to a bank account, is so subtle it often happens incrementally without our being aware. That unconscious heart-transfer of trust is the "deceitfulness of riches" warned against in the gospels (Matthew 13:22; Mark 4:19).

The person who tithes proves by his systematic financial obedience that he believes he will be better off with that 10 percent returned to God's hands as instructed. Thus, he begins to prove—with actions, not words—that he believes God is a real being whose word means something. But the person who does not tithe believes that is all just too thin to act upon, and he will be better off if he keeps it all.

Let's take a closer look at only a few of the many teachings on this issue. We'll begin with examples that serve as warnings against keeping everything for our own use. (Unless otherwise noted, I will be quoting the New King James Version of the Bible.)

In the Old Testament book of Haggai, the Jews, after a long dispossession, return to Jerusalem to rebuild the temple of God. Eighteen years later, they are living in Jerusalem in their own rebuilt houses, but God's temple still lies in ruin—and they are having problems. God sends a prophet named

FINANCIAL PLAN 1

Haggai to reprove and instruct them. Haggai tells them since they have looked after no one but themselves, God's judgment has frustrated their labors. God's prescription for breaking the privation and frustration they are struggling under is to honor God with their finances.

Here's what God, through Haggai (1:2-11), has to say about their hoarding:

> *Thus speaks the LORD of hosts, saying: "This people says, 'The time has not come, the time that the LORD's house should be built.'"*
>
> *Then the word of the LORD came by Haggai the prophet, saying, "Is it time for you yourselves to dwell in your paneled houses, and this temple to lie in ruins?" Now therefore, thus says the LORD of hosts: "Consider your ways!*
>
> > *"You have sown much, and bring in little;*
> > *You eat, but do not have enough;*
> > *You drink, but you are not filled with drink;*
> > *You clothe yourselves, but no one is warm;*
> > *And he who earns wages,*
> > *Earns wages to put into a bag with holes."*
>
> *Thus says the LORD of hosts: "Consider your ways! Go up to the mountains and bring wood and build the temple, that I may take pleasure in it and be glorified," says the LORD. "You looked for much, but indeed it came to little; and when you brought it home, I blew it away. Why?" says the LORD of hosts. "Because of My house that is in ruins, while every one of you runs to his own house. Therefore the heavens above you withhold the dew, and the earth withholds its fruit. For I called for a drought on the land and the mountains, on the grain and the new wine and the oil, on whatever the ground brings forth, on men and livestock, and on all the labor of your hands."*

"Lord of hosts," a term of military usage—the Lord of armies of both seen and unseen resources—is a name for God in his most powerful attribute. When this term is brought forward into New Testament Greek, the name becomes *Pantokrator*—the Supreme Ruler—one from whose power of decision there is no appeal and whose decrees, regardless of all opposing circumstances, *will* become fact.

In other words, it refers to ultimate authority. Sometimes also translated as "almighty," it is used to encourage and remind people that God alone is all-powerful to act on their behalf. No matter how impossible, perplexing, or unalterably dire their circumstances may seem to be, one word from Him can change the course of their lives from frustrated to fruitful, through means impossible for them even to conceive of.

Now, do the financial problems these people were experiencing—one setback after another taking what little they had—sound familiar? Well, they did to me, and I took that warning literally. I decided, if I were going to get ahead, *I could no longer afford to keep everything I earned.*

In many other places, the penalties for expending everything on ourselves are also made clear. And, in many other places, the rewards of giving are spelled out for our instruction and benefit. For the sake of brevity, I will choose only a few.

Christ spoke of compensation as a very real force in Luke 6:38 when he said:

> *Give, and it will be given to you: good measure, pressed down, shaken together, and running over will be put into your bosom. For with the same measure that you use, it will be measured back to you.*

And, once again, there are also warnings in Luke 6:46–49:

> *But why do you call Me "Lord, Lord," and not do the things which I say? Whoever comes to Me, and hears My sayings*

and does them, I will show you whom he is like: He is like a man building a house, who dug deep and laid the foundation on the rock. And when the flood arose, the stream beat vehemently against that house, and could not shake it, for it was founded on the rock. But he who heard and did nothing is like a man who built a house on the earth without a foundation, against which the stream beat vehemently; and immediately it fell. And the ruin of that house was great.

Both men had a plan for their future. Both men invested and labored. Both men succeeded and built great houses. Then, both men faced trials over which they had no control—but only one man had divine protection. And the rewards for his labor remained with him.

In the book of Malachi, the last book in the Old Testament, compensation is revealed as a direct act of God's interposition in our affairs. God is directly discussing his predetermined response to those who honor him with their money. (Interestingly, this verse concerning the tithe is the only place in the Bible where man is instructed to put God to the test.) In Malachi 3:10–11, God describes the ultimate outcome of financial obedience:

> "Bring all the tithes into the storehouse, That there may be food in My house,
> And try Me now in this,"
> Says the LORD of hosts,
> "If I will not open for you the windows of heaven
> And pour out for you such blessing
> That there will not be room enough to receive it.
> And I will rebuke the devourer for your sakes,
> So that he will not destroy the fruit of your ground,
> Nor shall the vine fail to bear fruit for you in the field,"
> Says the LORD of hosts;…

Remember, their crops were the modern equivalent of our business affairs. To this day, abundant "crops," both agricultural and figurative, are required for our survival and prosperity.

We can also infer a reverse result from spending the tithe on ourselves: no divine interposition and no divine protection from devouring circumstances. Though our labors may produce wealth—and, certainly, many wealthy men and women have never tithed—they remain outside divine protection, blessing, or favor. In fact, God says they are thieves! Malachi 3:8–9 says,

Will a man rob God?
Yet you have robbed Me!
But you say,
"In what way have we robbed You?"
In tithes and offerings.
You are cursed with a curse,
For you have robbed Me,
Even this whole nation.

And, in Deuteronomy 8:18, it is written,

*And you shall remember the L*ORD *your God, for it is He who gives you power to get wealth, that He may establish His covenant which He swore to your fathers, as it is this day.*

God wants to help us find our wealthy place! And wealth does not refer only to money. Wealth is any place and time you are living a satisfying life, are content and are enjoying a lot of precious moments.

Proverbs 3:9–10 very clearly instructs that giving will lead to financial blessings and divinely inspired ideas and connections:

*Honor the L*ORD *with your possessions,*
And with the firstfruits of all your increase;

FINANCIAL PLAN 1

So your barns will be filled with plenty,
And your vats will overflow with new wine.

Speaking for myself, I am now certain that God commands tithing so he may bless both the one receiving the gift *and the one bringing it*!

This, then, is the bottom line of why I tithe: by sharing with others, I am making the first expenditure of each dollar an investment in my future, and I am doing it out of a heart of compassion and gratitude. Just as kernels of corn produce corn, financial seeds sown in gratitude with a cheerful heart produce a harvest of financial blessings with peace: "The blessing of the LORD makes one rich, And He adds no sorrow with it." —Proverbs 10:22

> But a lifetime of tithing has kept me calm when facing many an uncertainty.

I am talking about a lifestyle of sincere, grateful giving that touches every dollar of increase that comes to you with an attitude of expectancy toward your future.

Now, this does not mean there are not battles; it does mean that, in my battles, I have had an all-powerful ally present through all my ups and downs. And individual effort—consistent and enthusiastically directed—is still required to produce increase whether one tithes or not. And troubles will come to all of us.

But a lifetime of tithing has kept me calm when facing many an uncertainty. A well-reported story has surfaced for years in financial publications about Sir John Templeton, of the Templeton Growth Fund. One of the wealthiest investors who ever walked Wall Street, Mr. Templeton was asked at an investment conference to name the one best investment he had ever made. He replied, "Giving," to the startled reporter.

But Where Should the Tithe Go?

Perhaps by now you are convinced that tithing is indeed important in your quest for financial independence. If so, your next question is likely, "How do I determine to whom to give?"

Actually, it may not be a question of whom because giving God's tithe directly to individuals is never permitted in the Bible. The tithe goes to God's house. But I have to acknowledge that my books are not written only to Christians and that men and women of other faiths, and of no faith at all, may want to begin a lifestyle of compassionate generosity. I think the principle is observable everywhere that what we send out comes back.

So, I would suggest that, should men or women of no particular faith wish to add compassionate generosity to their lifestyle, they choose organizations doing work they care about. More often than not, money given directly to individuals simply acts as a buffer between them and the circumstances with which God has surrounded them in an effort to shake them and wake them to wiser choices.

I do give to individuals when I feel prompted to do so, but I do not use the tithe, and I am careful of when I do it. I have learned that God's liberating work is not helped by misguided interference when He is trying to get someone's attention to make wiser choices. For illustration, I will recall a couple of instances when I did give money directly to an individual in need. In one, a woman with eight children, several of them adopted, lost her husband suddenly in a tragic accident.

In the other, as I stepped out of my truck to head into a store, a young man approached, offering to sell me his work tools. I asked, "Why are you selling your tools? If you sell your tools, how are you going to make a living?" He responded,

I'll think about that later. My wife has a drug problem, and we have a young son. She has taken what little money we had

FINANCIAL PLAN 1

and left us, and I need to get to my parents' home in Illinois so they can watch my son while I try to find work up there. My son is upset and wants to see his grandparents. I can't keep working down here in Atlanta and leave him alone every day.

I could tell this was not a hustle. I saw a young boy, maybe six years old, in his truck, and this young man was sincere and in a bad spot not of his doing. I rarely carry more than a few dollars on me, but, this particular day, I had five hundred-dollar bills in my wallet. I can't remember why I had such a sum on me, but it was probably by divine appointment.

"You will need those tools to make your living when you get to your parents' home in Illinois," I told him as I handed him all five bills. "This should get you both there and allow you to buy some food along the way."

He looked at me in disbelief as his eyes welled up with tears. Unable to speak, he nodded his head in a *thank you* gesture, slowly reentered his vehicle, and drove off.

When I got home, I underlined the first three verses of Psalm 41 (New Living Translation, NLT)—quoted earlier in this chapter, but in a different Bible version—and put his name beside them:

> *Oh, the joys of those who are kind to the poor!*
>   *The* L ORD *rescues them when they are in trouble.*
> *The* L ORD *protects them*
>   *and keeps them alive.*
> *He gives them prosperity in the land*
>   *and rescues them from their enemies.*
> *The* L ORD *nurses them when they are sick*
>   *and restores them to health.*

I claimed those verses for myself, and I have had more than one occasion to have need of them. That act of Christian compassion gave me great confidence in the protection promised in those verses. And let me add, $500 was a lot of money to me then. That was years before the circumstances of my own life had become abundant.

Despite that story, I must issue a strong caution: *you should not be moved to give away money, not even to a charitable or religious organization, solely based on a convincing appeal.*

You can't give away money based on an emotional appeal or a good story any more than you can invest in Wall Street intelligently that way. You have to be on your guard before you *invest* your money, and you certainly have to be just as skeptical and do just as much due diligence before you *give* money away. A convincing personality making an appeal for money while emotionally charged photographs are being shown is no more a basis for an intelligent charitable decision than it would be for a proposal to buy stocks.

As a case in point, one day my daughters and I saw an ad on television for pet rescue. The photos were heartbreaking. Who does not want to help save an animal from cruelty? But here's the catch: I happen to know the organization running that ad has never built one animal shelter—not one. Oh, until that fact became public knowledge and then one was built to get the heat off them. They are top-heavy with high salaries and, at best, are a political activist group.

You simply cannot accept appeals for support at face value. So, please, have *personal knowledge* about any organization's inner workings before writing a check.

Every human has a body, a mind, and a spirit. Supporting those whose life work is to provide for your spiritual needs is no different from paying for a college education to improve your mind or for a medical doctor or chiropractor to care for your body.

However, you cannot afford to rely on the personality of the man or woman making the appeal. At the risk of sounding crass, practice makes perfect, including emotive appeals to raise money. Charitable giving is big business, and due diligence applies everywhere and to everyone.

One more thing: if giving to a religious organization does not appeal to you, plenty of other charities are doing work worth supporting. In fact, probably my entire offering—which is any amount of money I give away above the tithe—goes to charities and not religious organizations.

Let me share with you three of my personal choices in charities to help you get a clear idea of what I look for in a charitable organization before I part with my cash.

Dream House for Medically Fragile Children Inc. in Lilburn, Georgia, was one of the most deserving organizations I have ever known of. A beautiful lady named Laura Moore started it. As a nurse on the Eggleston campus of Children's Healthcare of Atlanta, Laura saw many severely impaired and medically challenged children abandoned at the hospital when their parents were overwhelmed.

A child needing that level of twenty-four-hour care was just too much for some parents to cope with. So, after admitting their children to the hospital, they would move away, leaving no contact information. Other children were simply beyond the ability of any family to care for and were sent to nursing homes as wards of the state.

She saw these children languishing alone, left without a place to live, a family to love them, somewhere to play (or anyone to play with), and nowhere they could call home, nowhere they could belong. As heart-wrenching as this is, it happens in every state in the country. The last time I saw any numbers on it, my home state of Georgia had over 950 such cases.

With the blessing of her husband, Michael, and their children, Laura decided she was going to quit her job, complete the 501(c)(3) application, raise the funds to buy a home, renovate it to accommodate the healthcare needs of the children, and begin to take these kids into a real family environment. She called her vision Dream House for Medically Fragile Children.

Laura was a selfless and tireless champion for these children, children who could do nothing to help themselves. For many of them, the first time they had ever been outside a care facility was when they were brought to Dream House. In some instances, as a result of severe isolation, they had to be taught how to play! Besides housing these children, Dream House also arranged adoptions, family training, respite care, and foster care.

Unfortunately, expenses outstripped donations and the original plan had to be modified. Dream House began using the specially equipped home to provide weekend respite care for families with special needs children. Often it was the first time in years the parents had been able to have a single day together away from caregiving duties. Dream House also provided training resources for agencies and families dealing with this issue of medically fragile children all across the country.

Sadly, Dream House, after many years of effort, finally had to close its doors due to lack of money. I still wanted to tell you about it as an example of why we need to be supporting local charities that will never be seen on television. I applaud large ministries and large charities that reach out to the world with millions. But I believe our giving should include, and perhaps start with, the needs in the cities and counties where we live.

Just ten miles from where I live is a "tent city" in the woods. Women who have been abandoned and have nowhere to turn occupy some of these tents with small children. Why should I drive past them to send my charitable money to the other side of the globe just because a phone number on the television makes it easier?

Remember: There probably is someone in your city doing a work just as deserving of your support.

A second 501(c)(3) charity I wholeheartedly championed was The Autism Foundation of Georgia, formerly CADEF, the

FINANCIAL PLAN 1

Childhood Autism Diagnostic and Educational Foundation created by Martin and Marjie Truax of Marietta, Georgia. When their second son, Justin, was born, very few medical professionals anywhere in the country had even heard of autism. As Justin began to show signs of developmental problems, Martin and Marjie had to be persistent just to get a diagnosis. Only through their relentless determination was a correct identification of his disorder eventually made by an out-of-state doctor. Nowhere in Georgia could families dealing with an autistic child get an accurate diagnosis, and what to do afterward was not yet understood by anyone.

That was until Martin and Marjie came along. They began a foundation to make accurate diagnostics and proven methods for getting these children to their highest possible level of function available to families dealing with autism, regardless of their ability to pay.

Talk about taking on a load! Where do you even start when the entire medical community does not even yet understand the illness? They even had to explain that autism was not an "artistic" disorder! That was now more than three decades ago.

Today, thanks to The Autism Foundation of Georgia, a beautiful building on the prestigious Emory University campus here in Atlanta, Georgia, is dedicated solely to the diagnosis of and support for Georgia families dealing with this disorder. The Justin Tyler Truax Building hosts the Emory Autism Center and is named in honor of Martin and Marjie's son. It is one of the most advanced centers in the country dedicated exclusively to the diagnosis and treatment of autism.

Their foundation also helped to create model classrooms where specially trained teachers bring these kids up to their highest possible level of function. And parents receive counseling to guide them through their bewilderment and distress when they learn of the lifelong challenges they must face.

The Truaxes worked tirelessly without pay; indeed, a great deal of their own savings provided for the seminal needs of this organization. Martin and Marjie are my heroes and my friends. After the professional community began to provide many of the needed services to the families dealing with autism, the foundation was gradually able to pull back, except for a few private fundraising events. What a remarkable success story. There are similar charities in your town or state that need your help.

My wife and I also send a check each month to a local Christian-based charity that helps addicts in recovery and men released from prison, many with no place to go but under the local bridge. They are taught the disciplines necessary to return to productive and responsible lives.

These men are provided with a place to live, clothes and personal care items, counseling, and transportation to and from job interviews, and, once they find work, transportation to work, if needed, until they are accustomed to independent living. And, most important, someone who has successfully returned to society ahead of them mentors these men.

Only God can know how many lives they are saving and how many futures are being changed by this organization. They are 100 percent dependent upon donations to provide their help.

Again, someone in your community will almost certainly be sacrificially serving in similar programs.

I find it particularly important to support local charities like Dream House for Medically Fragile Children, The Autism Foundation of Georgia, and proven, moral-based, local drug and alcohol rehabs. These organizations have no access to television and no ten-thousand-name mailing lists. They must have your support and mine to survive.

I cannot emphasize this enough: once you have decided to make giving a part of your plan toward financial independence, please move beyond being a typical television-watching "couch donor." The sacrificial and selfless ministries contributing to the welfare of your own community will probably never be advertising on a TV screen.

Putting to Work the Law of Increase

When it comes to giving, almost everyone's first thought is, "I can't afford to help anyone else; I'm barely making it myself." I felt exactly that way. But tithing is not a suggestion for those who can afford it. It is God's command to everyone, rich and poor. If you net $1,000,000 a year, then $100,000 of it is God's. And, if you net ten cents a year, one penny is God's. God is equitable.

> If everything you can do hasn't been enough for ten years, what makes you think the next ten years are going to be different?

If you want to see a change in your own circumstances, you might want to think of your choices in a different way. Maybe, instead of being responsible for every solution yourself, you decide to take on a managing partner for ten percent of your earnings. The definition of insanity is to keep doing the same thing over and over again while expecting a different result. If everything you can do hasn't been enough for ten years, what makes you think the next ten years are going to be different?

Yes, you may have to make adjustments and sacrifices to get your finances in order, but, for me, tithing was step one. Is it really any wonder that my life has prospered? Yes, most of us are used to thinking the money we have is ours to spend as we please, but, in the long run, committing it back to God is, in my opinion, the most important step you can take to secure your future.

Let me ask you a few questions. Are all your children well? Mine are. But I know quite a few who can't say that. Do you have a job? One of my best friends has been unemployed for a year, and it isn't his fault. Do you have a warm home with food in the cupboard and clean water available on-demand and a dry bed to sleep in? Most of us will drive past someone nearly every day that does not. Can you even imagine the desperation that you and I have been spared?

No matter how hard you have worked for what you have, you did not have any control over which country and what circumstances you were born into. You owe a debt of gratitude for that. Life is not that way for a lot of people, and it could have been very different for you and me.

> God will respond to every step we take toward Him.

God doesn't need you to give him your money; *you need to give it.* The only meaningful way to say "thank you" is to help other human beings who were not so fortunate. "[I]nasmuch as you did it to one of the least of these My brethren, you did it to Me." —Matthew 25:40

Put the law of increase to work in your own life! Why not? Consider this: even if there were not a God in heaven, how could you do anything which would bless you more than to get your twenty-four-hours-a-day focus off me, my, and mine and help someone else in need, even if only with a little of your time or a few dollars? If you absolutely can't sow money, then sow an equivalent amount of time. God will respond to every step we take toward Him. You will see it if you are looking.

And remember, all seed has to be left in the ground and given time to grow. Don't pull your seed out before the time of the appointed harvest just because it doesn't produce a crop in a day. Trust the promise of Luke 6:38: "Give, and it will be given to you: good measure, pressed down, shaken together, and running over…" Notice the future tense: "it *will* be given to you…"

If you say, "You are using God," so be it. You are entitled to your point of view. If you don't believe in God, or if you do not believe in the Judaic or Christian view of God, you are equally entitled to your opinions.

FINANCIAL PLAN 1

I do not claim to be an authority on the mysteries of life. I can only state that, for me, it has boiled down to this:

I believe in God. My conception of him may not be perfectly accurate; how could it be? But I believe that God is, and that God is a good God! I believe he wants to help us.

After all, what kind of God would create a creature and then look for an opportunity to judge and condemn him? That's not the kind of God I pray to.

And I believe God inspired men to write the scriptures to help us avoid pitfalls and live a life of peace and fellowship with Him.

Concerning money, over and over God says through the scriptures that, if we want his help, we invite his participation by honoring him with the first 10 percent of our income. Well, I knew I would need His help. I was insufficient on my own. So, I made the decision to follow the instructions, as I understood them—and I have never regretted it.

And I would not stop now, even if I found out that every belief I have is wrong. There is something warped, selfish, and morally repugnant about being well mentally and physically—blessings you had nothing to do with—and never giving a dime to bring hope to anyone else. Take away the spiritual nature of this conversation and that is still the bottom line.

I am writing these lines during the Christmas season. Please, watch the movie *A Christmas Carol* (and I strongly recommend only the version from 1951 starring Alastair Sim). That movie is more eloquent on the subject of how giving produces rich living than all my written words.

I have now explained the tithe principle and its nexus to well-being and wealth as well as I can. Nowhere else in this book will we look at the topic from such a spiritual point of view.

RICHES BEYOND THE BLING

Perhaps fewer of you are still reading this book, but, as your reward, you are about to be treated to one of the most intensely practical, life-changing, commonsense collections of advice about financial independence you will ever read.

Because what I write about—everybody can do.

CHAPTER 7
FINANCIAL PLANS 2 AND 3

Money is a health issue. Ready money is a health issue.

As I told you earlier, I was twenty-four when I wrote down my first financial plan, and it included…just one step. However, as I also wrote earlier, when I made a new habit of each objective, I gradually added steps to my plan. My goal was financial independence, and I was constantly asking myself, "What should I do next? What is the next most logical step?"

In the next three chapters, I will take you through the rest of my plans—those steps I took to bring me to where I am today, living a life of blessing and financial independence.

Perhaps all these steps won't be ones you will choose, or a different order will make sense to you. That's fine. But once you've taken a look at my remaining financial plans, you'll know everything you need to in order to find your own path to financial independence, which is why you're reading this book.

Financial Plan 2

1. Tithe.

2. **Save 10 percent of your net income. Put enough money in a separate savings account to provide for your lifestyle for three months if all income stops.**

Where All Wealth Starts

Every harvest begins from a seed, and that includes a "harvest" of money. Taking a portion of what you earn each week and putting it into your own bank account is the starting point of all personal wealth. No matter how much is earned, the money will disappear without the consistent discipline of keeping a set amount of it off-limits from spending. Remember: as we talked about in Chapter 2, money resists being accumulated. It's slippery and will not be held by someone with weak hands.

Also remember the second of my *Thirteen Keys to Financial Independence* from Chapter 2, *How to Achieve Financial Independence:*

Money is a health issue. Ready money is a health issue.

Because health is so important, your first new goal—after the tithe—should be to sit down with a pencil and paper and find ways to reorganize your life to begin to save 10 percent of your net income. This should include thinking of ways to earn more as well as spend less.

Simply make up your mind that you are going to make your "grip" stronger when it comes to money. If you are thinking, "No way I can save 10 percent," then save *something*.

As a policeman in the early 1980s, I was earning very little. Still, I had the department payroll administrator hold fifty dollars out of each week's paycheck. I placed it in a separate account (more on that in a moment), and I never touched

FINANCIAL PLANS 2 AND 3

it—even though, for three years, I could not afford a spare tire for my personal car.

For two years, my only splurge was one six-pack of beer purchased from a convenience store down the street from my apartment. Which had to last a week, since the $2.75 it cost was *all* my weekly discretionary income.

It doesn't seem like saving fifty dollars a week could ever make much difference, does it? I didn't think it would at the time myself. But, when I left the police department, to my surprise, I had saved $14,000.

That was enough to make the down payment for my first home. I later sold that home and made a profit of $11,000, which I rolled into the down payment for our next home. When I sold the second home, I made thousands more. I then used all my accumulated equity to qualify for the purchase of my third home, in which we currently live. Today, the value of that property is well over $1,000,000!

None of this would have happened if, twenty years earlier, I had not saved fifty dollars a week when, by any standard, I could not afford it. But fifty dollars a week saved for a few years provided the down payment for my first home.

See? You *can* do *something*!

I read of another man who, beginning in his childhood and continuing for twenty years, paid for every purchase with dollar bills, and rolled and saved all his change. He made the down payment for his first home from the change he had saved!

If you have to start with saving less than 10 percent, then just do what you can. However, do not dismiss the need to put aside at least 10 percent of your income. The first few thousand dollars will be the hardest money you ever save. But it gets easier after that. Keep at it. *Do not settle for saving any less than 10 percent of your net income.*

Savings Must Be Kept in a Separate Account

Money is like water; you can't pour it all into a common account and still keep a portion of it safely separated for a particular purpose. So—ALWAYS—keep your savings in a separate account.

And then keep your hands out of the account. That is the only way to handle something as slippery as money. Your savings account for collecting three months of living expenses is for emergencies only.

Whenever I set aside money for any particular use (such as paying off a certain debt), it goes to that purpose and no other. Even today, with a considerable income and no debts, I still use envelopes labeled Christmas Gifts or Vacation Money for those planned discretionary expenses. If a little money comes unexpectedly into my hands during the year, I'll add it to one of those envelopes.

That may sound childlike, but it's simple and it works. In the beginning I used this method to keep me from reaching into my savings account. Now I do it because it has worked so well for me over the years.

Bottom line: a few years after I started tithing, once I had adjusted to living without that first 10 percent, I decided to start saving. At that point, I made up my mind to put aside 10 percent of my net income until I had enough saved to carry me for three months if my income totally stopped. These many years later, I can still remember how much more secure I felt—and what a great sense of accomplishment I had—when I finally had enough money in the bank to carry myself without a paycheck for three months!

By the way, whenever I would receive an occasional windfall—for example, an income tax refund—I tithed on that,

> Keep your objectives small enough so you can see progress.

too, and then the rest went into my separate savings account until my goal of three months' margin was met.

Obviously, six months of savings is better than three (more on that later), but I found saving six months of living expenses too daunting a task in the beginning. There was just something about deciding to save enough money to live on for three months that seemed doable. I mentioned earlier that humans are impatient, and the need for money seems overwhelming compared to early-in-life income. Keeping my objectives small enough so I could see progress helped me immensely during that period of my life.

Think about this: once you set aside three months of savings, you will be in better circumstances than 75 percent of the people around you. And here's another eye-opening fact: only 40% of Americans have $500 to $1000 to cover unexpected expenses!

After you save enough for three months of expenses, you can decide for yourself whether or not to add more to it. As I was fairly confident of my ability to maintain my income, I settled on three months and, once that was reached, moved on to the next goal.

Financial Plan 3

1. Tithe.

2. Put aside three months of living expenses in a separate savings account.

3. **Protect your family from the most severe uncertainties of life: illness, death, and disability. Purchase medical, life, and, if practical, disability insurance.**

Medical

Life is unpredictable, so it is important to insure yourself against all kind of events that, if they occur, you cannot recover from on your own.

That makes medical insurance a priority. After all, hospitalization, even for a few days, is expensive. The need for medical care can arise without any warning and threaten years of savings. Uninsured medical expenses can put you in a bind for a long, long time. Over 60% of all bankruptcies in the US are caused by unforeseen medical bills.

So, single or married, you'll be wise to get a major medical policy to protect your savings from significant medical events. If your business does not provide major medical insurance, look into a plan for individuals and find one you can afford. You may want to do what I do: self-insure normal expenses by choosing a high deductible to keep premiums reasonable.

Life

If you have dependent children, life insurance with a large death benefit is the second most essential insurance to obtain.

Life insurance is often purchased by the wealthy for investment and estate tax reasons, but, early in life, buy it only for the death benefit. You will need your money in too many other places to be making life insurance payments disproportionate to your means and your risk of death.

And it *is* easy to get carried away with enticing presentations and to overspend when buying life insurance. So, to get the amount of coverage you need, you will probably have to purchase a simple, level premium, renewable, term policy. Term life insurance—which pays only in the event of death—is affordable.

The most important thing is to buy enough. One million dollars of life insurance may sound like a lot. However, if your dependents receive that payout and put it away at 5 percent

FINANCIAL PLANS 2 AND 3

interest, then after taxes on the interest, the proceeds will only provide about $3,000 a month income.

So life insurance won't replace all your income, but, at a minimum, enough should be purchased so the surviving spouse can pay off the home and place the remainder at interest to make the car note and keep the family's medical insurance in force. The instinct for self-preservation is strong, and people can usually find a way to make it if you leave them that much.

Consider preparing written instructions for your mate on how the money is to be used. To suddenly come into a million dollars or more can itself be a stressful event. My computer has a folder in *My Documents* labeled "In the Event of Death." I update it each year with contact information for the people I know I can trust to help my wife with the insurance money, should that become necessary.

Life insurance proceeds should never be put at risk. Pay off the home, then use the money that is left to buy more income. How? This is a time for professional counsel. Perhaps, with guidance, the remainder could go into a utility stock fund and/or a managed income fund and a bond fund, all of which should provide reasonable yield. Certainly, I would think twice about investing it all in bond funds. Bonds move inverse to interest rates: when rates rise, the bonds already issued lose value to compensate for the change in rates.

Your beneficiary should also be warned strongly against talking to anyone who contacts him or her about investing the money. *Life insurance proceeds are for survival only.* They are not to be put at risk chasing profits.

There is one caveat to what I have said thus far. If you are an above-average income earner, then looking into life insurance that provides enough coverage and also builds cash value inside the policy is one of the best investments there is. Why? Because the cash value can be drawn against tax-free and the money deducted from the amount given to your beneficiary upon your death. It's like having a tax-free emergency fund or retirement income supplement.

I am not an expert, and all these things are fluid and change over time with changes to tax laws. Which is why you should have a seasoned professional you can trust to refer the surviving spouse to in the event of need.

Disability

The thought of being disabled is so remote to most of us, and disability insurance is so expensive, that the purchase of a disability policy is usually not part of a household budget. However remote, still it is only prudent to protect yourself against the possibility of being temporarily or permanently disabled by an accident or injury if it is financially possible for you to do so.

You may not be able to afford as much disability insurance as you would like to have, but something is better than nothing. So, if you have the means to do so, purchase enough to cover the house and car notes if you are sidelined for a couple of years. That way, your family would be able to keep the house and car. And, if possible, make the disability payment enough also to keep the life insurance and medical insurance in force. That's a lot of worry off everyone if all they need to do is keep food and utility bill money coming in while you recover.

This is costly insurance, and, if after looking into it, you find that you can't afford it, you may have to skip this one for now. I have had disability insurance since my thirties, and I have never needed it—and hope I never do.

A Reminder of the Importance of Plans 1, 2, and 3

Are you tempted to dismiss the simplistic financial suggestions I've made so far? Yes? Then let me ask you: do you have three

FINANCIAL PLANS 2 AND 3

months of savings tucked away? No? Well, then how about just three *weeks* of savings? No again? So, if an accident put you out of work for two years, how would you pay the bills? What would you live on?

I do know what I'm suggesting may seem simplistic, but what percentage of the adult population is doing it? Not many. Not many at all.

And how many are *financially independent*? Even fewer.

So, let's review what we have covered so far.

In your first step toward greater control over your finances and—eventually—the increased wealth and financial independence you seek, you tithe. In other words, you invite God to begin to move on your behalf into your work/business/financial affairs.

The truth is, consistent giving can help you conquer one of the most universal fears, the fear of poverty, and give you poise in tough times. How? Because you will have good reason to believe you will not be alone in trials and that there is an infinitely wise power working behind the scenes on your behalf to bring you out safely.

Next, you prepare for the unpredictability of life by setting aside three months of savings in a separate account. You have a bed to rest your body on at night. Well, a three-month savings account is like having a pillow to rest your mind on at night.

Just these first two steps alone are a big accomplishment. But, in step three you add to that by insuring yourself against serious reversals.

With these things done, you will be ahead of 90 percent of the men and women around you, including many who make a lot more money, but mishandle it.

More truth for you: everyone needs to set aside enough savings to give him or her some breathing room. *A well-funded savings account is more important than owning a home.* And we all also need to be insured against large losses due to injury, illness, or death because any of these events, no matter how unlikely, can threaten our ability to keep ourselves or our families sheltered and fed.

Doesn't it make sense to do these important things first, even before you purchase or furnish your home or take an expensive vacation? Financially speaking, this is no more than getting to first base. Think of it as financial kindergarten.

Yet I am continually astonished at how many people never even make it to financial first base because of an entire lifetime of upside-down decisions. They may have big houses and nice cars and be good neighbors, but, if you were allowed to see what is really going on, they have almost nothing saved and are under loads of debt, and tithing is out of the question.

What? Save 10 percent of my income? I wish! I can hardly save a hundred bucks a month.

And give away 10 percent of my income to honor God? You must be on something stronger than oxygen! I haven't been doing so well. I don't see why I should owe him anything.

A financial partnership with God sounds like the talk of a religious fanatic to them. But who is the fool? They live on the edge and struggle to keep everything under control by their own power. It is a life with no reason to believe there is a force bigger than them to help, no margin for error—and a constant undercurrent of stress.

I hope you are beginning to see more clearly who is truly being wise.

Not that there won't be setbacks.

I remember when my wife and I had finally saved $14,000, exactly the amount needed to support us fully for three months. And then our home's plumbing needed major repairs, the refrigerator expired, the washing machines for both dishes and clothes quit working, the car broke down, and other expenses I can't even remember occurred—*all in the same month!*

FINANCIAL PLANS 2 AND 3

Never before or since in my entire life has anything similar happened. It went from being shocking to just ridiculous. Can you guess how much it cost to straighten everything out? Yep, $14,000. We had to start over from scratch. But at least we had it. Because of our savings, it was disappointing, but not an emotional crisis.

We are all going to have setbacks in life, but the other side of the same coin, hardly ever considered, is this: if unexpected events can set you back, *equally unexpected events can and **will** occur to push you forward—if you do not give up.*

Even though it is easier to remember the disappointments, *just as many unforeseen events will occur to aid you over the years*—like an unexpected cash gift from parents, or an inheritance, a bonus, or some other serendipitous happening that cannot even be thought of before it occurs.

All this can be your story, too, if you remember the importance of Financial Plans 1, 2, and 3. Think of them as your essentials for financial wellbeing.

But you're seeking more than a backup plan and relief from an emotional crisis. You want financial independence, and so we continue to add steps to our plans.

CHAPTER 8
FINANCIAL PLANS 4, 5, AND 6

There is simply no such thing as a sixty-second result or a certain path to wealth.

I spent nine years achieving my first three goals; now, in this chapter and the next, let me introduce you to the remaining plans that led me, over thirteen more years, to true financial independence.

During those years, were my family and I sleeping on the floor and eating off shipping crates? Absolutely not. Our standard of living was growing throughout this process, and yours can, too.

Financial Plan 4

1. Tithe.

2. Put aside three months of living expenses in a separate savings account.

3. Get properly insured.

FINANCIAL PLANS 4, 5, AND 6

4. **Pay off the credit cards.** (Note: Steps 3 and 4 can be reversed.)

Once you have some money saved and are prudently insured, it is time to reach for second base: use every dollar you can find to *get rid of all credit card debt.*

You might ask, "Shouldn't I pay off my credit cards before buying insurance?" That is up to you and what you are comfortable with. If the credit card bills really bother you, then you might want to switch Financial Plans 3 and 4 and pay those cards off before getting insured.

I chose to buy the insurance first. Here's why: if there is a crisis, the credit card companies can get paid when they get paid, but, if you are sidetracked by an illness or an accident while without insurance, the downside could be much more serious. But I will concede that, knowing myself, if I had been behind to creditors who were harassing me, I too would have dealt with them before buying insurance.

As it was, my wife and I did not have a great deal of consumer debt when we married, but I considered one dollar of consumer debt one dollar too much. We had $4,000 in credit card debt between us (which, in today's money, would be more like $10,000). In just a year or two, with both of us working, we finally had no debts except one car note and our home mortgage.

How do you pay off those cards? I did it one card at a time because spreading out small additional payments over several cards is slow and discouraging. It really helps to see the balance on at least one card completely disappearing.

Paying off the card with the highest interest rate first is what is recommended, but I paid off the card with the lowest balance first and then worked up. For me, it was more encouraging to see one get paid off, cancelled, and cut up just as soon as possible.

This is important: as you get each card to a zero balance, call the credit card company, and *close the account*; otherwise, the account remains open even though you may have cut up the card. An active credit card account can be a temptation to replace the card and use it again, and, even with a zero balance, the open credit line counts against your credit score. An open credit card account is also vulnerable to misappropriation by increasingly sophisticated internet crooks.

Today, to keep credit available to me in case of emergency and to maintain a good credit score in case of need, I use no more than two personal credit cards and one credit card issued to my company. I never put any charge on them *unless I already have the money to pay for it*.

There are no exceptions.

Credit cards are not to be used to fill in the gap when you don't have enough money. I have a friend who used them just to fill in for food and other necessities he did not have the cash for. As always, credit as a "temporary solution" was the wrong solution from the beginning. He bankrupted, owing credit card companies a great deal of money.

Credit cards should be used only when cash is impractical, such as for internet purchases, or when you want the protection to dispute charges a card affords, such as when buying something made to order or when a purchased item is to be delivered at a future date.

My wife and I use cash for routine shopping, and it is humorous how often a sales clerk seems confused when she asks, "Which card will you be using today?" and my wife replies, "I'll be paying with cash."

Make a permanent decision to live without credit card debt. Talk about your life getting better! Just wait till you owe *nothing, nada, zip* on even a single credit card! No statements coming each month? Just imagine...

FINANCIAL PLANS 4, 5, AND 6

You may have to make some lifestyle changes to get there, and it may take a while, but freedom from credit card statements is more than worth it.

Now, with that monkey off your back, where do you go next?

Financial Plan 5

1. Tithe.

2. Put aside three months of living expenses in a separate savings account.

3. Get properly insured.

4. Pay off the credit cards. (Note: steps 3 and 4 can be reversed.)

5. **Pay off your vehicle.**

Is it unreasonable to suggest you set a goal to live without a car note? I don't think so, and I'll tell you why.

You and I both know you cannot function in modern society without an automobile. We also know a car is going to last about ten years if it is cared for. Therefore, if it is reasonable and practical to prepare for an unknown potential expense—which you do when you purchase insurance or put money into a savings account—is it not even more reasonable and practical to prepare for a known major expense which will definitely occur every ten years?

You may be thinking,

> *Whether I agree with his point about tithing, I understand it; the need for savings and insurance I certainly agree with, and I'm with him 100 percent on eliminating and avoiding credit card debt—but no car note? Now he's gone too far.*

> *There's nothing wrong with having a car note and a house note.*

I agree. There is nothing wrong with having a car payment. That is not the point. We are talking about financial independence here, right? My own intention—and my suggestion to you—is to find a way to live without *any monthly debt*. The question for me was never if I should get rid of car payments; for me, the question was, "*How* can I get rid of car payments?"

Cars are expensive. If better plans are not made, they are going to put you right back into serious debt every time you buy one. So, once you have no credit card debts, make a plan for providing yourself with a new vehicle every eight to ten years without financing it.

Before we were married, my wife had purchased a new Chrysler, and she still owed several thousand dollars on it. I was driving a twelve-year-old Buick, but it was paid for, clean, and in good condition. To me, the car was beautiful, and I enjoyed it. Once our credit card debt was eliminated, we decided to work together to pay off her car. Within a couple of years, we had paid it off.

As with everything else we did, once we set the goal, we put everything we had toward it, including a surprise gift of money from the parents (we got to pay them back later with surprise gifts from us!), income tax refunds, and anything else that came our way.

But once that car was paid for, I decided to plan a way to pay cash for our future vehicles.

If you keep your vehicles well maintained, they last a lot longer than five years, which is probably how long most people finance a car for. Once a vehicle is paid for, assuming you drive it if it is safe and reliable, often it can last five more years after you've paid it off. So, once your car is paid for, *if you will keep making the payments to yourself*, when it comes time to buy the next car you can pay very close to cash.

FINANCIAL PLANS 4, 5, AND 6

And, after the first ten-year period, you can buy a new car every five to seven years and pay cash or very close to it, because you keep making the payments for the next car to yourself, even though you paid cash for the car you are driving.

By the way, until you are well off financially, consider buying a used car that is a couple of years old. Let someone else pay for the depreciation and you instantly save thousands of dollars.

Following this plan, which requires only that you make one car last ten years, you never again need to make significant payments to a creditor for an automobile. If you think this idea novel, you might be surprised to know I once heard it reported on Bloomberg News that, in China, the savvy, saving Chinese *pay cash for 90 percent of the new cars purchased!*

The last vehicle I bought was a new Ford F-150 pickup truck. I had the money to pay cash, but the Ford Motor Company was offering a low interest rate to move their vehicles, so I agreed to finance it for two years. Although I made payments on the truck, I knew that any time the need arose, I could write a check to pay it off.

It all goes back to driving one vehicle a little longer than normal, and, after the payments stop, making the payments for your next car to yourself ahead of time, *before* purchasing the next vehicle.

You might ask, "Why go to all this trouble when a car loan is so easy to get and already in the household budget?" Here's why:

1. Money-savvy men and women often do the opposite of what the majority of people do. They are opposed to adding thousands in credit charges to the cost of a depreciating liability that will be worth less than one-fifth of what they paid for it in just a few years.

2. You always want to keep as much margin in your life as possible. Margin equals peace of mind. Car notes remove margin.

Even if you drive your current car for less than ten years and can set aside monthly payments for only a few years, anything you can do here will greatly reduce the size of the payments on the next vehicle. Eventually, the thousands of dollars in interest you now give the creditors will be in *your* bank instead of theirs. Much more importantly, you will be reducing debt and stress.

Avoiding payments on a depreciating liability is always savvy, and planning for expenses before they arrive is just good common sense. Planning for expenses and providing for them before they arrive will force you to keep your budget in check. To do nothing and then borrow money you knew long ago you would need is not proactive financial planning.

So, it may be out of reach for you now, but reducing or eliminating your need for a car note will become an achievable goal once you have paid off your credit cards and made the last payment on the vehicle you are driving currently.

Financial Plan 6

1. Tithe.
2. Put aside three months of living expenses in a separate savings account.
3. Get properly insured.
4. Pay off the credit cards. (Note: steps 3 and 4 can be reversed.)
5. Pay off your vehicle.
6. **Raise your savings to cover six months of living expenses.**

FINANCIAL PLANS 4, 5, AND 6

Once you have no credit card debt and no car payment, it is smart to set a goal to raise your savings account balance to cover six months of lifestyle expenses rather than three. If you decide you will pay off your credit card debt but continue to finance your vehicles, then move this goal up one step.

> Nothing real is ever quick and easy—except for getting ourselves into trouble, financial and otherwise.

The truth is, the great majority of setbacks will be resolved before six months have passed, so this new level of margin will really help provide peace of mind.

For the majority of us, this plan is workable, though certainly not quick and easy. In fact, nothing real is ever quick and easy—except for getting ourselves into trouble, financial and otherwise. *Private Choices, Public Power*, the fifth book of the Common Sense for a Prosperous Life series, will dig into this.

While on the treadmill yesterday, I heard two radio commercials one right after the other. The first one closed with, "This program will give you results in the first sixty seconds. Call now!" And the next one began, "If you knew of a way to become wealthy that was quick and easy, would you do it? Well, there is a way! With our program…" and so on, ad nauseam.

As I listened, I thought, "The great circus organizer P.T. Barnum was right: there's a sucker born every minute. You can't sell anything anymore unless it promises instant results."

Life has never been easy, not since the first human walked this planet, and it's not likely going to be easy for you. But I am convinced the price of moving forward is always less than the price of going backward. You pay for failure every day of your life—and the price goes up a little every year.

Or, instead, you can make the sacrifices over a ten-or twenty-year period needful to win your freedom from creditors, and then every day of the rest of your life will be that much easier. No matter where you are financially right now, *from this moment on*, you can decide to turn your thoughts to getting out of debt.

There is simply no such thing in life as a sixty-second result or a certain path to wealth. When I first made up my mind to become financially independent, I was driving a police car and rarely had more than twenty dollars in my pocket or my bank account. But those facts had nothing to do with the truth that, at that moment, I was just as free as any other person on earth to accept that as my lot in life or to make a decision to find a way to improve my financial condition, however long that would take.

If you can make payments to a finance company for a car, then you can certainly make them to yourself—*if you* have the desire to start doing things differently. If you can eventually get rid of all credit card payments and car notes, then the money you used to pay those creditors can be applied against the principal on your home and you can pay it off fifteen years earlier—*if you* are that determined to win your freedom from the money lash.

You are probably years closer to your freedom than you suspect. Just set your mind to the task.

Then, as you reduce debt, you can gradually increase the amount budgeted for food, clothing, dining out, and vacations. And these "little things"—such as a generous weekly grocery budget, opportunities for travel, a comfortable nest egg of savings, and a life free of stress—will bring more long-term pleasure and happy memories than the grandeur of a fine home at the top of your price range or a new car that is the envy of your friends.

All it takes is your decision, and a plan.

Read on for your next step.

CHAPTER 9
FINANCIAL PLANS 7 AND 8

It is amazing what you can do with one single thought if that thought is allowed to take root in you.

Small steps are the way to reach any big goal, but especially one as easy to break down into those small steps as getting out of debt.

Try to think like a batter in a baseball game. You don't need to hit a home run; just get on first base. Save some money for emergencies; then get some insurance to protect yourself or pay off a credit card. These things alone are a huge accomplishment, no matter how long they take. After all, probably five out of ten people you meet have close to nothing saved.

To get to second base, pay off your lowest balance credit card, and then keep at it until you have paid off all your credit cards. Even if this takes five years more, *it is tremendous progress.* Remember: even though it is usually necessary to have a credit card, do not use it for any reason unless you already have the cash set aside to pay for what you are buying when you charge it. *It is better to go to bed hungry than go to bed in debt for the food in your belly.*

You're on third base when you get rid of your car note. It took years for my family to get to that point, but it was worth it. No matter how long it takes you, having no credit card debt and no car payment will put you in a rare group—and get you very close to stress-free living!

As you progress, a few sensible rewards are recommended, too. My wife and I certainly rewarded ourselves along the way. We went to eat at better restaurants. I occasionally gave my wife money to shop for an attractive outfit from one of the top-end boutiques in our home city of Atlanta. We began to take vacations when we had the ready money.

But we never re-dug the hole we were climbing out of. We refused all temptations into new debt. We refused to exchange real freedom for a financed counterfeit of the "good life." The comfortable life we have now is real; not a dime of it is financed. We quite literally bought our life back from the creditors.

> All achievement begins with a decision to change things and then taking your next step in that direction.

Even if you only succeed in eliminating every debt but one modest car note and the mortgage, that much is real accomplishment and I would be so proud for you! If a high-school educated cop taking home $175 a week can decide to do it—though, at the time, I could see no way I could ever earn more or save anything—what's your excuse?

All achievement begins with a decision to change things and then taking your next step in *that* direction. In the next plan, we dig in for the run to home plate—and freedom for life!

FINANCIAL PLANS 7 AND 8

Financial Plan 7

1. Tithe.
2. Put aside three months of living expenses in a separate savings account.
3. Get properly insured.
4. Pay off the credit cards. (Note: steps 3 and 4 can be reversed.)
5. Pay off your vehicle.
6. Raise your savings to cover six months of living expenses.
7. **Pay off your home.**

Why not set a goal to pay off your home? Does just the thought of it seem impossible to you? Let me tell you something about the word "impossible." It is amazing what you can do with one single thought if that thought is allowed to take root in you.

All human history teaches us that unseen, previously unknown, powerful forces wait behind the scenes of your life, ready to aid the man or woman who becomes passionately focused on a single idea. Christ pointed to this eternal truth when he said, "…[A]ll things are possible to him who believes."—Mark 9:23, NKJV

Walt Disney risked everything he had to make Disneyland a reality. A statement by William Arthur Ward, twentieth-century author and speaker, was often attributed to Disney, for obvious reasons: "If you can imagine it, you can achieve it."

The story is told that, when Walt Disney World Resort in Orlando, Florida, was celebrating its grand opening, a man on the platform with Mrs. Disney remarked to her, "It's too bad Walt didn't live to see this." Mrs. Disney replied, "He did see this. That is how it got here."

Don't let the fact so few people really own their homes or that you see no way to pay yours off—or maybe even to buy one—cause you to dismiss it as a possibility. For one thing, you have a lot to do before you tackle that large a goal. Don't ever let a *distant* objective overwhelm you.

But let me ask you to do this: just let it remain in the back of your mind. Think about what it would feel like, without thinking about *how* or *when*. For now, let yourself imagine owning a home—and not having any payments. Simply let the idea germinate without you feeling pressure to do anything other than consider the possibility. Life can be full of surprises when your mental "wheels" chew on something long enough.

> Life can be full of surprises when your mental "wheels" chew on something long enough.

My Rationale for Paying Off Your Home

Up to this point in discussing how to handle money, my advice has been valid no matter what your circumstances. The benefits of tithing, saving, insuring yourself against reversals, and getting rid of consumer debt apply to everyone.

But a home is different. Having a place to live is not like buying a car or a couch; it is not consumer debt. And, unless you are rich, a home must be financed.

Paying off any debt early is an act of caution. And there are times when it is prudent not to pay off debt, such as when building up your first savings account (which is more important than paying down debt elsewhere) or when buying real estate to resell for a profit as a business venture.

But your own home is not something you purchase to make a profit on, though that may happen. It is your most essential material possession—a place of shelter from the world, a place to care for your family's physical and emotional needs. So, any threat to your home is as serious as money trouble gets.

FINANCIAL PLANS 7 AND 8

That means a home that is paid for is a tremendous emotional comfort.

Even though you may think yourself able to get a better return on your money elsewhere, you might pause to consider that "man shall not live by bread alone." (Matthew 4:4, NKJV). So, by now, I am sure you will not be surprised by what I am about to say:

Once you have saved some money and paid off your credit cards and your car, I think you should set a goal to own your home outright.

More than four hundred years ago, Shakespeare wrote, "Delays have dangerous ends." And a few years before Shakespeare's plays were published, poet John Lyly penned the same warning more forcibly: "Delays breed dangers."

Here's something I wrote during the real estate sub-prime loan crisis of 2009:

Yesterday, I saw a report on CNN that one in ten homes in the United States were in foreclosure or late on their payments. One in ten! And the rate of foreclosures is accelerating. At the time of this writing, we are in the middle of a global economic crisis the smartest men and women on earth did not see coming—and it won't be the last one.

Though the rate of foreclosures, for now, has returned to normal, I am only in my early sixties and already looking back on the *fourth* major national or global financial crisis I have lived through. Huge numbers of men and women lost their jobs in each of these crises, and entire sectors of the economy failed. Why do delays *breed* dangers? Because no one knows the depth of the challenges they may face in the future. We only know—or should know—they will come.

And reader, *come* they will in your lifetime, too. A lot of people do lose their homes, many through no fault of their own. I personally know such people. But remember: the financial crises will come, and also will eventually *go*.

Each of the crises I witnessed looked almost permanently debilitating…and yet every one of these crises were completely past within five years. Each of my friends who had things turn so wrong they lost their home, completely recovered, or were even better off within five years. They went on to own other homes and live productive, happy lives.

In other words, *we all have a tendency to give money trouble too much weight*. There is no money trouble in the world that must mean the end of your hopes. So, when economic events turn for the worse in your life, just repeat this truthful saying: "Survive for five and then I'll thrive!"

Am I giving you a blank check to go ahead and experience money troubles? No! But when setbacks come, they will also go—especially if we have been committed to reducing debt during the good years.

I have a friend who owned a booming business for several years. Instead of paying off debts, he and his family traveled and built a luxury home. Hey, if you can afford it, why not? I wondered if he were overreaching during those good times, spending most of his income on lifestyle. Of course, I didn't ask; that was none of my business. But I privately had misgivings when he spoke of his business debts for expansion, and the things he was spending personal money for. When we talked finances—which two men, each with his own business, will do—he never mentioned eliminating debts.

During those same boom years, I traveled some with my family, too, and I spent a little money. But my focus was on capitalizing on the favorable circumstances by paying off our home, not building a bigger one.

Why pay off a home if you are earning plenty and the future is bright? My friend can answer that question for you now. He made a common error. When times were good, he built his lifestyle around his income, assuming his improving circumstances were the new permanent norm for his life.

They were not.

When the home building market collapsed—which his business depended upon—his income shut down as if someone had turned off the faucet, and he was holding millions in expansion debt. He could have expanded in smaller steps and, as the debt was reduced, expanded again, all the while whittling away at his mortgage with his personal income. In hindsight, he should have.

He ended up closing some of his stores, but the damage done was insurmountable. Business did not pick up in time to save him. Had he made a priority of paying off all debts—*including his home*—his situation, though challenging, would have been far different. He would at least have had something to show for those good years. As it was, his own home had to be sold, and for far less than he paid for it.

The general business conditions he was caught up in, which are none of his doing, are not the point. This is: unless something is eternal, it will change. As I said in Chapter 2, it is not good years or bad years that are normal—it is **changing conditions**. My friend did not take that into account in his financial planning, and neither do a lot of other smart people.

Everyone will have setbacks, but they are certainly more manageable when one's home is not at risk. I described my friend's situation because it illustrates that, even if your income is large, changes can occur *that cannot possibly be anticipated*. And, no matter what you do to produce income, you are not the exception.

I am not being negative. I am being a dispassionate observer of the world I live in. The years of "go to college, pick a career, make your house note without any problem for thirty years, and retire with a pension at sixty-five" *are gone forever*.

Frankly, if difficulties come—and even if they don't—it is better to own your home outright rather than renting it from the bank. You don't think it's rent? Miss a few payments and see who really owns your home. Until you pay for it, *it's rent*.

And if this can happen to the wealthy, wouldn't the warning apply even more earnestly to those with lesser incomes?

Contrast my friend's story with my position. I also own a home improvement business, so I too had a sharp decrease in income during the most recent downturn. But, since I had used all my years, good and bad, to eliminate every debt possible, including my home mortgage, the poor economy had no real effect on my family's lifestyle.

What would a life like that be worth to you?

Doesn't that kind of lifestyle make greater sense as the objective for your years of health and labor? It does require a specific intention; a larger income alone will not do for you all that you expect. There must be an equal zeal to eliminate personal, consumer debt—debt that does not produce income—any and all of it.

My friend had a grand home, much more impressive than my own, and he *had* a much larger income, but I *own* the life I have built, and to get here I had to make different choices. As much as I used to marvel secretly at the rapid growth of his business, I suspect he would trade positions with me now if he could. Personally, I would rather go up a little more slowly and never have to worry about coming back down. Wouldn't you?

I'm not being a Chicken Little, the children's storybook character always looking for the sky to fall on him. My self-evident observation that—unless something is eternal it will change—doesn't just apply to the ending of good times. As I've already mentioned, bad times pass too, and things begin to improve, and good times can and do get even better. My point is that we can control a whole lot more of that than we accept responsibility for when times are good.

FINANCIAL PLANS 7 AND 8

I work hard to improve my life, but I don't kid myself: *life is too large for me to control.* I expect good things to happen, but the best way to be prepared—and to do what I can to assure that good things *do* happen—is to plan for the unexpected.

When it comes to your most important financial objectives, you should consider well that you are in a race against time and chance.

It is not usually changes we can predict that send us reeling. It is some turn of events no one could have anticipated.

During the last crisis, a famous Wall Street brokerage firm went bankrupt. That would have been unthinkable just six months earlier. Twenty-five thousand employees not only found out they had no more paychecks coming, but that the stock they had accumulated in their company was worthless. And, if they had a retirement tied to employment contract obligations, it too was gone. Twenty-five thousand families, no doubt many near retirement age, blindsided!

The news reported that these sophisticated men and women were crying while they emptied their desks of personal belongings. The "unthinkable" had just happened in real life *to twenty-five thousand families.*

When you have a goal as important to your welfare as paying down debt, and you have the means to make progress toward your goal, you had better use those means for exactly that purpose. Dissipating your opportunities can have consequences.

A home isn't yours when you buy it.
It is yours when you have it paid for.

At one point, while perusing a quarterly report on economic conditions written by my friend Martin Truax for his clients, I saw that according to the *Campbell Real Estate Timing*

Letter (which follows trends and pricing in real estate) almost two-thirds of the homes in the United States with outstanding mortgages had equity of less than 15 percent of appraised value. That is *asking* for trouble. You are supposed to have more equity than that from your down payment!

If you are buying a home and you cannot afford a legitimate down payment that leaves you with some money left in the bank, you are starting wrong. I have no idea why so many have an aversion to renting. It is not "throwing away money" if it gives you time to get your feet under you financially.

I have always been the type of individual who rests only after the work is done. I consider nothing done until all is done. That's a sound and productive policy all the way around, but especially when considering home ownership. The financial institution that holds your mortgage can take away your home over missing the last payment. **When it comes to owning your home, count it as *nothing done* until *all is done*.** That's the safe way. I urge you to follow my example and act with diligence. Set a goal and make a reasonable plan to get completely out of debt ahead of schedule.

Answers to Some Common Questions

What if this is not the home I intend to remain in?

Then the equity you build in the current house will roll into the next home, reducing the amount you need to borrow.

What if I don't own a home yet?

That's perfectly okay. Renting is fine and, in many cases, preferable, I think. Owning a home is not worth a life of stress. When you rent, there are no maintenance issues. Once you own, you will find that proper maintenance of the lot and structure is much more costly than you thought, which is why so many owners choose to let their homes deteriorate.

FINANCIAL PLANS 7 AND 8

So, if you can't make the payments *and* keep up with all the needed maintenance, you can't afford it. And that is true with anything.

How much should I spend on a house anyway?

Once you are ready to buy, you will probably have to borrow the money. But, before you decide how much you can afford for a house, here's a word a friend shared with me some years ago that was a winner in the *Washington Post*'s "Style Invitational" (often erroneously associated with Mensa, an association for persons of high IQ).

> *Cashtration (n.): The act of buying a house, which renders the subject financially impotent for an indefinite period.*

This humorous but cynical definition makes my next point well. *Why do we shop for a bargain on a new blouse but pay retail for a house?* Find a motivated seller or buy a fixer-upper and work to improve the home on weekends. But find *some* arrangement that will give you equity at the closing table.

And remember this: the mortgage is only a fractional part of the expense of owning a home. You must take *all* house-related expenses into account. Add the house note, insurance, taxes, and a monthly allocation of at least 15 percent of the house note for maintenance. The **total** should be no more than 20 percent of your take-home pay.

Now, lenders will tell you the house payment with taxes and insurance can run about 25 percent of your take-home pay in a proper budget. But, when you add maintenance and utilities to that, you will be spending over 30 percent of your net income on housing—not including anything for furnishings.

What does that leave for food, transportation, insurance, routine medical expenses, savings, clothing, contingencies, and so on? Not enough, I assure you.

Trust me: walking that tight line is not for the mentally bright. Government statistics regard any household with total home expenses of 40 percent of income to be financially distressed. No kidding!

Some years ago, Paul Harvey News related in a radio broadcast that government statisticians reported 7,500,000 households that particular year had total home expenses of *over 50 percent of household income*. I suspect family life suffered in those homes, don't you? What in the world were those people thinking? Owning a home is just not worth that price.

> A home is not a status symbol; it is a place to live.

Don't let your enthusiasm and a creative mortgage broker meet each other when you are looking for a home. The outcome will not be to your benefit. Think instead about the chaos and heartbreak that seven million homeowners went through when they lost their homes to foreclosure in the 2008-2010 mortgage crisis fallout fueled by the "creative" mortgages approved in the mid 2000's. You don't want this to happen to you.

Listen to me instead: 20 percent or less for all direct and indirect home ownership expenses combined—*period*. It *is* attainable if you find a distressed seller or buy a home needing some work you can perform yourself.

Start with the attitude that "$_____ (no more than 20 percent of your take-home) is what the note, taxes, insurance, and 15 percent more for maintenance can total—tops," and then stick by it. Do some patient house shopping to find situations where you can keep the payment to that level.

And no adjustable rate mortgages, please. If your income does not grow as planned, or if unanticipated expenses arise, an increasing house note can become way too stressful.

FINANCIAL PLANS 7 AND 8

What if I've already overbought?

One of my friends who read a draft of this book before publication told me that doing so made him frustrated with himself. He said it became discouraging to realize he had already done a great deal wrong, and now, at fifty-three years of age, he was angry he had never been taught such simple financial thinking *before* he messed things up.

That frustration is not my intention. If you are already in over your head, please don't kick yourself. You can't hold yourself responsible for what you didn't know at the time the decisions were made. Just begin from where you are now and make sensible corrections when you can. In the fourth book of the Common Sense for a Prosperous Life series, *Unchain Your Brain,* you will find my thoughts about helping put your life on a higher path.

A home is not a status symbol; it is a place to live. Of course, it should be well kept and inviting, but its size does not indicate the value of the person in it. On one occasion I was telling a friend about a lavish home filled with investment grade art in which my wife and I were guests visiting with new friends. I think he felt I had become a little overawed with their wealth. And, being a successful man not unfamiliar with wealth and big homes himself, he made a remark meant as a discreet way of telling me to keep my feet firmly planted. He said, "Mark, some people are so poor that all they have is money."

Even if you can afford it, a large and lavish home is not necessarily where your money needs to be spent. And if you can't afford it…well, any home bigger than your budget is folly.

We all have been around people who think material things make others impressed with them. We know instinctively there is something wrong about that attitude in others, so let's resist it in ourselves too. We all prefer down-to-earth people who are comfortable to be around. They may have nice things, but they never go out of their way to make anyone aware of it.

Apparently, they know that considering any difference in cars or homes as representing real value is nonsense. We all admire that trait in the wealthy, but, if we got what we have by honest labor, it is okay for every one of us to feel that confident.

Once I was asking a bank for a line of credit. I invited the decision-makers to my home and took them on a tour. I then said, "People who want a loan often show you their fancy homes and their many possessions and assure you that, because of these things, your money will be safe with them. But I have just shown you the opposite of what you expected. Your money *will* be safe with me, not because of all the things I have, but because of all the things I can do without." I got the loan.

Riches Greater Than Money

I was present many years ago at a luncheon with a Medal of Honor recipient who had been a POW for five years. I regret that I no longer remember his name, but his storytelling was a real ministry. During his imprisonment, to busy himself, he made notes of what the men talked about while in captivity, a time when what is truly precious in life was in such sharp focus. Adjust your thinking to this bit of wisdom from him:

> *Your life is not made of the things you possess. Material things, beyond functional comfort, were a total nonissue with everyone. No one's status before the war made any difference at all in how we thought of each other. Your life is truly made of four precious things: family, friends, fun, and faith. And none of that costs much in money.*

And I add my voice to his on two points:

1. Unless you are super wealthy, your material welfare is made or unmade *by all the things you can do without.*

FINANCIAL PLANS 7 AND 8

2. **Family, friends, fun, and faith are the true *Riches Beyond the Bling*.** Don't lose them chasing more stuff.

Shouldn't I invest my extra money rather than pay off my home?

The right answer to this question depends on you. Income stability, business circumstances, personal goals, and the level of financial sophistication vary greatly from one person to the next, so there is no rule that fits everyone.

My sense is that, for the majority of us, it would be hard to argue against using some funds to prepay on the home first. Here are my reasons for your consideration:

1. Paying off your home *is* investing; if you define investing as allocating funds to provide security for your future.

2. If you are putting all your spare money into mutual funds, then I think you should consider paying off some debts along the way, including your home.

   How much money are you spending every year in interest on your house note? What is the interest rate you are paying on that note? Do you think you are going to get a *guaranteed* rate of return that is greater than that, year after year, on Wall Street? Probably not.

   One caveat: if you have an employer matching a good percentage of your contributions to a stock retirement plan, then by all means take full advantage of that first. It is not a matter of one or the other; you should do some of both. Adding just 10 percent more to your mortgage payment can do wonders over time.

3. If you are truly a whiz at something, or think you can be, then you may be right not to pay off your house debt first. If you have a real passion for investing or business and think you could succeed at it, you owe it to yourself to try. You can take your shot at it and prove yourself either right or wrong.

   But, for most of us, successful investing may prove more difficult than we had assumed it would be. Besides, just how much money will you really need once you don't owe anyone a dime?

   You might ask yourself which would make you feel better: a large stock fund balance or a home you own outright? Then act according to your own preference. Honestly, my suggestion is to accelerate the principal repayment with a portion and invest the rest.

4. If you borrow money for a home and pay it back over thirty years, you will probably pay for the home twice: once for the price of the home and the remainder to pay interest to the lender. That can amount to hundreds of thousands of dollars in additional payments for interest.

   I realize the interest is paid over many years and those years give other investments time to grow, but consider this: how much money do you have to earn to save enough, after taxes and living expenses, to invest as much as you are paying the mortgage lender in interest each year? A bunch—in reality, a ton of money.

   And there are no guarantees you will earn that kind of return in the market, or even that you will make a real profit at all, after factoring for taxes and inflation. During my lifetime there have been periods

FINANCIAL PLANS 7 AND 8

when the Dow Jones Industrial averages were little changed for many years. Every dollar you put toward principal on your home mortgage is reducing the carrying cost of that loan and will give you a guaranteed return of up to two times its value, *with no risk to capital.*

5. I would suggest, for the average investor—which means the majority, who know our own business but little about investing—we can make no better investment than to pay off our mortgage in half the original time planned.

6. Just two or three hundred dollars extra—paid by separate check, or via online if that's how you pay and noted "for principal prepayment only" mailed in with the mortgage payment every month makes a remarkable difference in shortening the number of years you have to make a house payment. Many mortgage companies will allow you to automatically stipulate an amount monthly for additional principal payment and then do a withdrawal from your checking account.

Do what you can. You will be surprised how much closer you are coming to owning your home outright as the years pass by.

And remember: as I said earlier in this chapter, and also in Chapter 2, it is not good years or bad years that are normal—it is **changing conditions**.

In the real estate downturn of 2008, I received a phone call from a homebuilder who wanted to know if I had a job for him. He had built hundreds of homes over the past twenty years but did not have his own home paid for yet. He was caught in the economic tsunami. Very likely he, and his home, ended up among the many casualties.

RICHES BEYOND THE BLING

Even celebrities who made millions of dollars a year in their hay day were caught in the downward mortgage spiral. Several lost their mansions to foreclosures, one a former world heavyweight boxing champion and the other a television personality for more than forty years.

Both men's income-producing years were long past, but they had each made many millions of dollars. The boxer was reportedly paid over $20 million per fight during the height of his career, and the television star made millions *every year* also, far more than either needed to have their homes paid for—and their homes were in foreclosure!

You, too, could earn a generous income for years, just as these men did, and end up losing your home. It may sound unlikely, but it can and does happen. Investments, deals, and plans can take sudden turns for the worse, as happened to these men, and cash can get tight faster than you can get out of the way. And believe me: if for any reason you can't meet your obligations, the lenders are coming for what they can get.

Be smart. When money comes under your control, use it to protect your vital interests first. That will make you a much better investor later. An investor who does not need his money to do anything for him can be patient and unemotional—and patient and emotionally neutral investors are at a great advantage.

Several years ago, I made the poorest investment decisions of my life and the value of my investments fell dramatically. My wife asked, "What are you going to do?" I said, "Nothing. We are out of debt and we don't have to have the money in the foreseeable future. I have made a regrettable blunder, but, if we don't panic, time is on our side."

So how do we apply this lesson to business decisions? If you choose to invest in real estate or in any other business which will require debt, I would still urge you to arrange the finances to allow for regular contributions to prepay your home mortgage. Meet with your banker and ask how much you would have to prepay on principal each month to reduce your note from thirty years to twenty. It will surprise you how little extra is required, as well as how much you will save on interest. If you have a fifteen-year house note, find out how much you need to add to the monthly payment to pay the home off in twelve years instead of fifteen.

That's all I'm talking about: do something proactively to reduce your house debt. Set that aside as your minimum prepayment out of current income before you determine how much free cash flow you have for doing anything else.

And, if you can't meet that low threshold and you still want to use all your free cash to spend or invest elsewhere… well, I wonder how prudent that is.

Every dollar you spend eliminating personal, non-income-producing debt *is* investing for your future. Once your home is paid for, anything you do after that is like building on bedrock.

Waking Up Not Owing a Dime!

There are two kinds of investors: experts who know what they are doing and the rest of us. The experts don't need any advice from me. They will make their own judgments for their own reasons. For the amateur, the safest path is to put that hard-to-come-by extra money to work for you in a way so it cannot be lost and protects your most precious assets first. To me, that means making it a priority to pay off your home early.

Depending on your comfort level with the idea, you might want to decide to use some—or maybe even a lot—of your extra money to pay off your creditors, including your mortgage; *then* invest the money you used to be giving the creditors. You will be a little older and wiser by then, a lot calmer with

> Every plan will have twists and turns.

your investments, and in a far better position, financially and emotionally, to cope with the occasional losses and lessons.

Here is one of the things I did right. A few years after my wife and I moved into our second home, my stepfather located a farm for sale in the beautiful hills of north Georgia. He wanted Tracy and me to buy into it with him. There was a nice home for us on the property and plenty of room where he and my mother could build their home beside ours.

I recognized at once the future value of owning this prime piece of land. Once again, this would set me back in my plan to have no mortgage, but I decided that the opportunity justified the expense.

We drew up the paperwork so our interests were protected in the event of my mother's and stepfather's deaths, and I secured a life insurance policy on my stepfather to allow me to pay off his interest in the farm if he died. Which, in fact, happened a few years later. Once we settled in, we started right back on our prepayment of principal—$500 here, $1,000 there—but, I swear, I thought I'd *never* get rid of my house notes!

Remember, if unexpected events can set you back, equally unexpected things can speed you forward—if you keep at it. *It is so important to keep faith in serendipitous events when the road ahead looks long!* And that is just what happened.

The business I had labored at for fifteen years—always a struggle—began to prosper as our reputation for quality and ethics began to spread, mostly by word of mouth. To my surprise, seven years after buying the farm, my home and the five acres it sat on were paid for. Two years later, the entire farm was paid for. I was finally free!

Waking up every day of your life knowing you don't owe a dime to anyone is so different. Difficulties still come, financial and otherwise, but they just don't have the same power over you.

As you know by now—based on my experiences if not your own—every plan will have twists and turns. Life is not black and white; at times, circumstances or personal judgment will lead you to alter your course. At some point, you may decide to assume some debt for reasons personal to you, or you may decide to take a chance and make an investment. That's fine. Just don't overreach and keep your focus on the goal of freedom from creditors.

Okay, I've made my case as well as I can for buying your home with the intention of actually owning it and taking modest steps to do so. As we approach the end of this book meant to help you learn how to handle the money you earn so it provides benefits for life, I will now share with you the final step I took to maximize our margin and peace of mind.

Financial Plan 8

1. Tithe.
2. Put aside three months of living expenses in a separate savings account.
3. Get properly insured.
4. Pay off the credit cards. (Note: steps 3 and 4 can be reversed.)
5. Pay off your vehicle.
6. Raise your savings to cover six months of living expenses.
7. Pay off your home.
8. **Set aside enough money to pay for next year's major expenses, including vacations.**

Okay, admittedly, we are getting a little far out there for someone just trying to get their credit cards paid off. But the thought to do this *never crossed my mind* until it seemed to me to be the next logical thing to do. When I was still loaded with debt, it would have been a misdirection of funds unless I had reason to believe the loss of my job was a real possibility.

But, because I followed the financial plans' I am sharing with you, about twenty years after setting the goal to become independent…well, I had no debt. Other than insurance and utilities, there was no one to write a check to at the end of the month. So, once you are out of debt, the goal of setting aside the money to cover next year's major expenses is completely reasonable.

Here's what I did: before I started spending or investing any excess funds, I set aside what I needed for next year's larger expenses. I figured out what those items were and what they cost, added them up, and, starting at the beginning of each year, I now set aside that much for the *next* calendar year out of my earnings before doing anything else. Whatever I earn afterward is ours to spend or invest that year.

For me, personally, this is probably the most mentally comforting of all my financial actions with the exception of owning my home. I start each year knowing the money for the entire year's expenses (the major ones anyway) is already set aside. Since quality of life is so inseparably related to mental comfort—at least, for me—not even investing takes precedence over maintaining this large cushion.

And this doesn't interfere one bit with how much money I have to live on, because this money would have to be raised and spent within twelve months whether I had it set aside or not. I had just rather put it away a little ahead of time rather than the way most people do it, which is to try to come up with the money they need when they need it.

So, you see, it is just a matter of a few months of timing, but it makes a big difference mentally. It just works for me.

Today, I continue to live one year "paid ahead." Understand, I do not set aside money for utilities and groceries—only for the larger expenses I will incur the following year, like vacations, property taxes, life insurance, school tuition for the kids, Christmas shopping, braces for the children's teeth, etc.

I set aside the money I anticipate will be needed for those major expenses during the following year, and then I spend or put into an investment account whatever I earn after that. As a result of the way I have learned to handle money, I have never had to take cash out of an investment account to cover unexpected bills.

One warning: once you are out of debt, you will begin to overspend without realizing it. That's almost automatic. It happened to me, and to every prosperous friend I have ever talked to about it.

Sure, spend some. But continue that same discipline you have learned. Now take most of the money formerly going to payments and fund your investment plan.

I'll talk more on this in the next book in the Common Sense for a Prosperous Life series, *Invest Like a Wealth Manager*. However, if you are not yet investing, you don't need to read that book yet. I suggest skipping forward to Book 4, *Unchain Your Brain*.

Getting the Things You Want

If you were to say to me, "Nobody can do this. If I live like this, I'll never get the things I want," I would reply, "If something is important to you, then make an exception for it, just as I did when I purchased a luxury automobile for my wife. As you make progress, you can begin to reward yourself."

Today, my wife and I enjoy a life full of material blessings. In fact, we have every material thing we really want. How many people can say that? We just did it in a more rational order than most.

Yes, to build this kind of lifestyle, we did have to wait on some things. Even when our current home was paid for, it was not furnished attractively, and the carpeting was dated and stained. But no one who visited cared. We were always told how time spent in our home and on our farm filled our guests with a sense that they had escaped from their world of cares.

They were not just being gracious; they were serious. The peace they sensed was and is very real. Despite all the drama that shakes the world from time to time, guests can actually feel something out of the ordinary when they are with us. *It is life being lived in the complete absence of stress!*

We live every day like that, and that peace is worth more—much more—than the few material possessions we have now accumulated. My wife and I never had a self-conscious thought about how we "looked" to someone else materially. The things we owned were kept clean and orderly, and that is all anyone has the right to expect of others.

Besides, you won't always have to do without the things you want. I am only suggesting there is a proper order to everything. And wisdom requires you should acquire the material things you want *only when you have earned them.*

When we decided it was time to furnish our home, we used one of the finest decorators available, James Taggart. He and his talented wife, Cynthia, have been close friends of ours for years. I told James, "I want this home to reflect the charm of the property which surrounds it and the goodness of God." I did not want a home that made visitors afraid to touch anything when they visited, and yet I wanted the feel of it to be abundant. When the time was right for us, James fulfilled the assignment perfectly. Our home is now as inviting as it is peaceful.

CHAPTER 10
BEYOND THE BLING

We each must decide, based on where we are right now, what we want to pursue with the rest of our life—and whether we are going to make excuses or make progress.

I want to do more than summarize what I've already shared, though I will start by doing that, too. But, mostly, I want to talk again from my experience about the obstacles we put in our own way and how to overcome them. And about the incredible peace and freedom that can be yours.

How Long It Took

Restated in brief, here are the eight plans I followed:

1. Begin to tithe. Invite God into your life, and then into your financial affairs, by making a lifetime decision to give Him that which He says is His alone: the first 10 percent of your net income. **I was 24 when I made this decision.**

2. Set aside enough money so, if your income stopped, you could support yourself for three months. **I was 28.**

3. Secure all needed insurance. **I was 33.**

4. Pay off all credit cards. **I was 35.**

5. Once that is done, decide if you want to pay off your car loans. For me, that was a no-brainer. I paid off our car. **I was 36.**

6. Once you have no debt but a mortgage payment, you may want to increase your savings account to cover six months of living expenses. Since I was self-employed with no risk of being fired—though I felt at great risk of going broke—I did not choose to increase my savings.

7. As the years go by, live well below your rising income, and use every dollar you can do without to pay down your mortgage. **I was debt-free, including my mortgage, by 45.** "Little strokes fell great oaks."

8. Set aside enough to cover your major expenses for the next year. Begin responsibly to reward yourself and your spouse. **I was 46.**

I am now in my early sixties; that means my family and I have already enjoyed more than a decade of freedom from an avalanche of bills at the end of each month and attained a reasonable level of financial independence.

Was it easy? No! Was it worth it? Yes! And it will be worth it for you, too.

Absence of Debt = Financial Independence?

Look at the eight steps in my financial plan. They all focus on getting rid of debt and protecting yourself from future debt, don't they? The obvious question is, does the absence of debt equal financial independence?

I think so; it certainly gets you a lot closer to it than most people ever get. There can always be exceptions—such as when you owe nothing because you have nothing.

However, realistically, if you have no credit card debt, a reliable car with no car note, and enough money in the bank to support your lifestyle for six months, *and* if you are employable and own your home outright, you are pretty much in control of your personal choices from there forward. I think someone in this position would be a practical example of the term financially independent.

And, as you have now seen, this is not a question of wealth but of many small personal choices, and of time. That means, financial independence as I have defined it is within reach of the great majority of people.

Thirty years ago, I left a promising career in law enforcement to join a roofing business that I knew I was ill-suited for. That was not particularly desirable to me, but it was the only opportunity that came my way. The business was foreign to my nature—and that is putting it mildly.

I began to pay down debts because, if my business collapsed due to my inexperience (as appeared to me was likely), I wanted the fall to be as short and painless as possible. I also wanted to have something to show for my efforts if things didn't work out, which seemed probable, so I took a no-brainer first step and set aside some savings.

After saving enough money to live on for three months, I decided my wife and I should pay off our credit cards and then get properly insured to protect us against large setbacks. When that was done, to my surprise, I was still in business.

I thought, "Well, I haven't gone bust yet. What should I do next so that anything I earn from here doesn't slip away?"

Once I decided what the next goal should be, my mind and my money were completely dedicated to that one thing until it was done. Every discretionary desire was made subordinate to that next goal. My intention was to make as much progress as possible in case my business did not survive.

I know that sounds negative, but I was just being realistic. The business did not suit me, and, at least on paper, I was not highly employable. I was a high school graduate who had enlisted in the military and then became a civilian cop. How exciting was that on a résumé?

In hindsight, that sense of vulnerability turned out to be beneficial. I knew I was a hard worker and a bright person, but I had to make it in business for myself or I was in trouble! I did not have the credentials or background to get ahead any other way. And, since I sincerely doubted my long-term prospects in that particular business, I was never even tempted to do anything but pay down debts with the money I earned. In other words, if I had to go back to police work, I wanted to be able to survive on a policeman's pay.

As it turned out, I was so driven by a sense of last resort, that, far from folding up, I eventually built one of the more successful home improvement companies in Atlanta, serving close to 800 homeowners a year with roofing, siding, window replacement, repairs, carpentry, and just about every other aspect of home maintenance.

Now, I don't want to give you the impression I recommend you use empty shipping crates for furniture and sleep on the floor while you run scared to get out of debt. I was diligent and focused, not frantic, in the pursuit of my objective to become debt-free.

So, don't think I lived an ascetic life and had no interests other than a cramped, blighted obsession with hoarding every penny. My wife and I were not surviving on cornbread and collard greens while I waited for the end to come.

Quite the opposite was true! My wife and I ate at progressively finer restaurants, started taking vacations when we could afford them, and even moved a couple of times into larger homes when the deal made sense. *Our standard of living grew—but at a much slower pace than our income.* Our obligations were not being *increased* with our rising income but rather *stripped away* with our rising income.

And we were very careful not ever to assume upon future earnings. In fact, I kept the attitude that future earnings could decrease or stop altogether, while, at the same time, I worked as hard as I could actually to increase them. In which effort, it turned out, I was generally successful. And, if we ever had a windfall, a portion was used to eliminate debt and the remainder used to buy something relatively needful, like furniture or clothing.

Taking on Debt on Purpose

For the sake of balance, I am going to share with you a few of the times I decided to take on debt or spend a good bit of money to do something my wife and I wanted to do. This is worth a few words, as detours may be in order with even the best of plans. And I also want to tell you about a time I missed a big opportunity because I was too focused on staying out of debt.

In about our third year of marriage, the neighborhood we lived in began to change for the worse, and we decided to move. I was patient and found a home in a beautiful area with a very motivated seller. The owner had been transferred, his home had not sold, and for a year he had been paying two house notes. His contract with the realtor had just expired. He accepted my first offer—the only one I could afford to make. With the purchase of that home, our mortgage indebtedness rose by $50,000, but I had purchased the house for 20 percent less than it had been listed for and we were able to relocate into a truly attractive subdivision.

After we moved, we had a lovely home, but it was empty. We had almost no furniture.

I told my wife,

> *This is the last home we will ever own. It's all we need. We have been denying ourselves for some time and have made good progress on our goal to pay off our debts. We have no credit card debt or car notes, and we're both still working. If we are ever going to furnish our home, now is the time, before we have children. Let's take a pause on paying down this new mortgage and furnish the house.*

First, I need to acknowledge I was mistaken about this being the last house we'd ever need. We moved again in a few years. Nevertheless, at the time, that seemed true, and so we began to furnish our home.

Of course, we decided to do so without borrowing, and it became hugely expensive. Once we began, I was totally focused on getting it furnished quickly and not going into debt for it. I was working at a frenetic pace to make every dime I could so we could get it done. I just wanted it paid for and behind me.

As far as stretching the bounds of sense for a discretionary expense, it was the most extravagant thing I ever did, and also one of the hardest.

Then I made a financial decision that turned out to be even more expensive than the furniture. As we were in the middle of our furnishing project, the new internet company America Online (AOL) went public with its first stock offering. I had never invested in a company's stock before, but I knew it was the beginning of a new era. Whether or not AOL managed its company well and made profits, Wall Street investors would be snapping up shares, forcing the stock price higher.

It occurred to me I should buy some AOL stock. I thought, "I should take $5,000 of this furniture money and buy some of that company's stock." Then I had a second thought—one that was to prove very costly indeed. "No, on second thought, I won't do that. I need every dime I can get my hands on to get this house furnished!"

Had I invested that money, within a few years, that investment would have paid me back for all the expense of furnishing the home with a good bit leftover.

After our home was finally furnished, we picked right up prepaying on the mortgage principal—without any help from the now astronomically priced AOL stock, which investment I had passed on to pay for a couch!

Lessons? It is generally a good thing to keep your focus on a single task and let nothing sidetrack you. But this time? It cost me greatly.

And there may be times when paying down debt should wait. It could be to make an investment or just to do something more important to you personally—as furnishing our home while we were both still working was to us. Learn from my mistake: do not become so set in stone about your goals that you miss an opportunity, especially when it is a perfectly clear one to you.

Here's another exception I made to my rule of "no new debt." After we had been married several years, my wife needed a new car. Instead of shopping for a bargain, I bought her a Jaguar. It was a couple of years old but had very low mileage and looked brand new. She had been as selfless a wife as any man had ever had, and I wanted to reward her. So, I put her into a nifty car and took on a car payment.

A few years later, when she became pregnant with our first child, we sold the car for one a little more practical. I never made any attempt to pay off the bank loan for the sports car. It was just a reward for her support. I never regretted the purchase, though the expense of paying for and maintaining the car was considerable. At the time, we had paid off a great deal of debt, and, as a result, my income could easily handle the payment without interfering with paying down the mortgage.

Paying Tuition for a Hard Lesson

Here is an example of an expense I did have reason to regret. After we moved into our current home, but before I paid off the mortgage, I lost a considerable amount of money attempting to trade in stocks. I now consider it tuition, but, when the losses occurred, it seemed more like the act of a fool.

I can remember one time in particular when I lost $24,000 almost overnight—about half of all the money we had! For weeks I could hardly sleep. My wife finally said to me,

> *Mark, the things you want to learn to do are hard. Every wealthy person we know made plenty of mistakes early on. That is the price of attempting difficult things. I know you can learn how wealthy people handle money and you will eventually succeed at it. I am not bothered by the loss of our money, and I am not going to lose a moment of sleep over it—and neither should you.*

And she didn't. My wife is my hero and quite a lady. She gave me permission to fail, as long as I was consulting her before making significant decisions, using my best judgment, and attempting to do something rational.

Important: *no spouse is obligated to submissively support a financial venture that is moronic.* Her or his future is at stake, too. I have never made a single significant decision, financial or otherwise, without consulting my wife to be sure we were in agreement on the appropriateness of the action. Honestly, I'll trust a woman's instincts over a man's logic any day!

This large financial loss relative to our means was a disappointing dose of reality. Even after years of study and my best efforts, I still had managed to lose a great deal of our money. It was painful, but probably fortunate in the long run.

As odd as it may sound, I think it is dangerous to experience early success. Caution is a great ally anytime money is involved. Successes are what we all want, but you will learn one hundred times more from your mistakes. Reading can only help so much. There is nothing like the pain of a few significant losses for teaching you what not to do. I've heard the shrewd Chinese reserve this blessing for their enemies: "May you have quick success!"

That bit of philosophy didn't help me feel any better at the time, however. The disappointment was intensified every time I thought about the fact that I still owed a lot of money on our home, and the money I had lost would have made a big difference. The money was gone, but my house notes kept coming.

That's why I always recommend that you "invest" in getting out of debt first. There just can't be any real regrets from doing that. **The loss of capital is always more painful than the loss of opportunity.**

Your Choice: Excuses or Progress?

We're heading into the homestretch now, but I can't close this conversation without a few warnings about listening to our own excuses. Our minds will always eagerly and convincingly present them. It is up to you to reject them. Indeed, your future is decided right there.

I can just hear some of you thinking, "Of course *he* could do this. He started young. He was not deeply in debt like I am. He found a way to work for himself and succeeded at it. I have already messed up too much, and I have too little to work with to even know where to start."

Well, I have thought the same things many times myself. Many times. When I saw the successes others were having—people who, in some cases, were years younger than I was and already millionaires while I was still struggling—it was only natural to feel that way.

There are ample reasons for any of us to give up if we are seeking them, and the quickest way to find plenty of excuses is to compare your life to someone else's. But you can't live my life and I can't live yours.

We each must decide, based on where we are right now, what we want to pursue with the rest of our life—*and whether we are going to make excuses or make progress.* That is the only choice you and I get to make. We all have to play the hand we are dealt and rise or fall from there based on our own actions. We don't get to be someone else. We don't get to start somewhere else.

Don't you think it looked like a mountain too high to climb to me, too? I was a policeman with a high school education and no idea what else to do. To move forward, as I've said before, I went to work in a business I did not like.

For the next sixteen years, I toiled under emotional circumstances I would not wish on an enemy. Every day I felt as if I were being asked to eat gravel with broken teeth. And all the while, other men of my acquaintance, younger men, made much more money while doing something they enjoyed.

One of my friends, a few years younger than I, started his business a year or two after I did and sold out for millions before I had paid off my cars! I can't tell you how much that discouraged me. For a year afterward, I could barely breathe under the weight of the self-contempt I felt for my apparent inadequacies as a businessman.

As years passed, I began literally to feel ashamed, even hopeless at times and ignored by a God that, if he existed at all, apparently had no interest in me. I had absolutely no idea things would ever turn around for me, or that, all these years later, the lessons I was learning would result in my Common Sense for a Prosperous Life book series. I had to find the grit to keep going through all those self-defeating thoughts. I still do. The odds against more than a few hundred people buying and reading one of my books is just as haunting, just as daunting, just as real, and *just as irrelevant!*

We can all make our own excuses and find reasons to complain and be discouraged. But what will that change for us? What new unexpected good can it bring to us? The only way for any of us to better our lives is to put blinders on when it comes to anyone and everyone else and then push through anything that is telling us, "This is all you get. This is as far as you can go. This is all you will ever amount to."

I discovered that, for the man or woman who will defy the inner voice of defeat, God will start arranging the *absolutely impossible* for us long before we are even aware that we have gained His attention! Don't tell me you have a wholesome desire for better and that God is just taunting you with it. I refuse to believe it or accept it.

Escaping from any confinement requires *a decision not to stay confined, long before you know of a way out.* You can dig out of a prison cell with a spoon if you want out badly enough and you will take the time.

Thomas Merton wrote, "Your life is shaped by the end you live for. You are made in the image of what you desire." I desired freedom from want for my family. I desired to stand on my own two legs without having to cringe before the decisions of others. I desired to become something more than I was at the time, a broke cop. And, as a husband and father, I considered it a sacred duty to do my best to fulfill my God-given role, as I saw it, to be a better provider, protector, and guide. And I was willing to put everything I had into winning that prize. Everything.

So, what do *you* want?

RICHES BEYOND THE BLING

Now What?

I don't mean to sound dismissive, but what good will it do you to read another book written by an internet wonder kid or a Fortune 500 CEO, other than providing entertainment?

I forged my life out of the common hopes and opportunities and responsibilities and roadblocks every working-class member of society finds around him or her, and because of that, this book is not about me: it is about your life going forward.

That's why I recommend, while you are working on the steps I have laid out for you in these pages, you should be reading a little bit every day from *Riches Beyond the Bling, Unchain Your Brain* or *Private Choices, Public Power* to keep you on track emotionally and mentally. Just put it within arm's reach and reread a few meaningful pages a day.

> Your life's path will cross those of a different caliber of people. Like attracts like.

You will also want to cultivate relationships with a few men and women of wealth who can counsel you. If you don't yet know anyone financially well-off, you will. Getting to the place where you are debt-free will take quite a few years.

As you eliminate debt and read to improve your people skills and financial knowledge, your life's path will cross those of a different caliber of people. Like attracts like. These people will be "kingdom connections," as my pastor, Jentezen Franklin puts it. And, very importantly, you will be becoming the type of person accomplished men and women are willing to help.

When I decided to find a way to a better life, I was a cop with a discretionary income of less than three dollars a week. My friends at the police department tried to discourage me from going out on my own. Some belittled me. One, a friend, or so I thought, shook his head in disdain and said, "So you're leaving to try to go into business? You've lost it,

Ashe." Crabs often don't like other crabs to crawl out of the catch pot ahead of them.

But I took the small opportunities life gave me and worked to make them better opportunities. And, even though I loathed reading, I read helpful books until reading became a habit. That one transformation took seven years during which I made no other visible progress, but I knew I had to grow in my knowledge outside of police work. I had to try to learn something about business and money because I knew nothing about either. And I had to learn how to *think* differently. My books can serve that purpose for you.

I couldn't even think of putting aside three months' living expenses when I was a cop. I could never even afford a second pair of tennis shoes so that I had one clean pair. I had to keep my focus on the next twenty dollars I could save, all the while looking for any way possible to go into business for myself. I never looked past the next goal, small as it was, because it would have been too discouraging.

So, I kept my focus only on the next step the entire way, and that step was always small enough I knew I could do it. For example, "Save enough money to live on for one week." I don't know that I have ever felt any more successful than when I finally saved my first $500! I still vividly remember my pride when I accomplished that feat. It was a princely sum to me.

What did I do after completing that step? I went out and bought a second pair of tennis shoes. I would walk down the hall of my small apartment three or four times a night and open the closet door just to look at my *two pairs of tennis shoes*! I could hardly soak up how rich I had become.

In other words, I have earned the right to tell you:

Don't look for excuses—look for a way!

Your Decision: One Step at a Time

During the Second World War, Churchill instructed the British navy to mine the English Channel. His admirals told him such an enormous task was impossible. He asked them if it was possible to put one mine in the English Channel. "Of course," they replied. He said, "Then put one mine in the channel, and then another, until the channel is mined!"

If you can't pay off all your credit cards next year, then pay off *one* credit card. Even if you work hard for ten years and succeed only at getting rid of your credit card debt and car note, *you will be ahead of 85 percent of the population.*

It may not be possible for you to pay off your home fifteen years early, but how about five years early? And be open for an inspired thought or an opportunity to do something new. *You don't need to see the whole plan for the rest of your life; you just need to recognize the next step when it is presented.* Divine guidance that leads us to unexpected progress may come through an intuitive thought or an idea that just strikes a note within you.

It does not matter if you are a policeman with no other skills, a single mother, an unemployed mechanic, or a millionaire seeking peace of mind and freedom from business pressures; you are not alone unless you choose it. There is a loving God who has the answer you need and knows the way forward before you ask. Even if you have to march through an emotional desert for a while, if you will keep going without abandoning your post, you will drink today's tears from champagne flutes tomorrow. And that is true no matter how bad it looks now!

> What alternative do we have but to take that next step from where we are and who we are?

You do not need to do everything that has been discussed in this book. It is only needful that you pick one goal that motivates you. You only need enough faith for *that one thing*.

Save five hundred dollars and put it in a savings account? Set aside fifty dollars out of every paycheck? Whatever it is, that is the only goal you need to write down or think about. Do it until it is a habit, then, do one thing more. That is all I ever did.

When I had three credit cards to pay off, I did not have a goal to pay off all three of them. I had a goal to pay off one, the one with the smallest balance. When I had no savings, I did not set a goal to save $10,000; I set a goal to save $500. My first long term goal to save enough money to take care of myself for three months if the need arose *took four years for me to accomplish.*

I started with small steps...steps that were achievable without feeling overwhelming.

As with Churchill's order to mine the English Channel, I focused on something I knew I could do, one step at a time. The entire task would have been too overwhelming even to contemplate.

Taking consistent small actions for a seemingly distant goal is called *faith*. Will it be enough? That is not knowable and is not a fair question to ask ourselves. For what alternative do we have but to take that next step from where we are and who we are? What choice do we have but to begin from right here, right now?

Shall we surrender the rest of our life to the current state of affairs? I think not! Facts can change. Facts *do* change. And, often, *we* change them...by taking small steps of faith.

If you and I are earnest and diligent and doing the most we can to improve ourselves and our conditions, taking into account where we are and what we have to work with, that is all we can hold ourselves responsible for.

There is a God who can make up the difference if we will turn our life over to him. But to surrender our dreams because the task seems too great or because we don't see any way it could happen is to hurl our future blessings back into the face of God. I didn't do that. And you shouldn't either.

CHAPTER 11
MY FINAL THOUGHTS…

*There are real riches on offer to you and me in this life…
lasting riches far more valuable than the
"bling" of glittery things.*

In *Chapter 2, How to Achieve Financial Independence,* I wrote these words:

Almost every person upon entering active life sets out with an intention to own his or her own home, to become debt-free, and to live without needless stress. That is, to become financially independent.

Few make it.

Few do make it, but I believe many more could and would if they were taught how in practical terms and encouraged to set it as a goal. I hope my life and my words can be useful to that end for you.

MY FINAL THOUGHTS...

Everything I have suggested to you in this book can be condensed into these two sentences:

1. Financial independence comes from doing everything you can to increase your income and then using every dollar possible to decrease your need for future income, by building a margin for safety and paying off your debts.
2. Quality of life is determined by personal character, financial margin, and self-restraint, not by the things that you possess.

What are the True Riches Beyond the Bling?

There are real riches on offer to you and me in this life… lasting riches far more valuable than the "bling" of glittery things. The true riches of your life are:

- Family, friends, fun, and faith
- Sharing a portion with others less fortunate
- Courage in the face of obstacles
- God has more for you
- Freedom from lack or financial stress
- Peace of heart and mind

What will your life be about? What is your decision?

ABOUT THE AUTHOR

Mark Ashe is the owner of a successful home improvement business in Atlanta. He and his wife of over thirty years have three grown daughters. They enjoy life on their 40-acre farm in the rolling hills of north Georgia, traveling with friends or with their daughters, and great meals shared with close friends. Mark went from being a policeman to debt free and financially independent by his mid-forty's.

Mark writes and speaks with compelling clarity on "common sense for the uncommon life." A wealthy financial adviser has described Mark's writings as "a PhD level course in successful living."

Mark's premise, and the proof of his life, is that an average man or woman can attain surprising success when the desire to do so is strong and the major decisions of life are made with a practical sensibility that his books bring to life through personal examples.

Connect at www.markashe.com

www.ingramcontent.com/pod-product-compliance
Lightning Source LLC
LaVergne TN
LVHW011902060526
838200LV00054B/4476